ALI TAYLOR

Ali Taylor's other plays include *S   .... (Polka
Theatre); *A Little Neck* (Goat & Monkey, Hampton Court
Palace); *Overspill* (Soho Theatre/Churchill Theatre, Bromley);
59 Cups (Topos Allou, Athens); *Cotton Wool* (Theatre503,
winner of the eighteenth Meyer-Whitworth Award); *Porcelain*
(Royal Court Jerwood Theatre Upstairs, Workers Writes
Festival); *Hive9* (Islington Community Theatre) and an
adaptation of Robert Westall's *The Machine Gunners* (Polka
Theatre, London). For BBC Radio 4, he has written *Cinders*
and *Eight Feet High and Rising*. Ali is an artistic director of
Buckle for Dust theatre company (www.bucklefordust.org.uk).

Ali Taylor

FAULT LINES

NICK HERN BOOKS
London
www.nickhernbooks.co.uk

A Nick Hern Book

Fault Lines first published in Great Britain as a paperback original in 2013 by Nick Hern Books Limited, The Glasshouse, 49a Goldhawk Road, London W12 8QP

Fault Lines copyright © 2013 Ali Taylor

Ali Taylor has asserted his right to be identified as the author of this work

Cover image: SWD (www.swd.uk.com)
Cover design: Ned Hoste, 2H

Typeset by Nick Hern Books, London

Printed in the UK by Mimeo Ltd, Huntingdon, Cambridgeshire PE29 6XX

A CIP catalogue record for this book is available from the British Library

ISBN 978 1 84842 376 3

Fault Lines was first performed at Hampstead Theatre Downstairs, London, on 5 December 2013. The cast was as follows:

ABI AHMED   Natalie Dew
NICK WEBB   Samuel James
RYAN GIBSON   Alex Lawther
PAT WILLIAMS   Nichola McAuliffe

Director   Lisa Spirling
Designer   Polly Sullivan
Lighting Designer   Tim Mascall
Sound Designer   Richard Hammarton
Audio-Visual Designer   Douglas O'Connell
Stage Manager   Naomi Buchanan Brooks
Production Manager   Michael Ager
Assistant Director   Amy Ewbank

Characters

ABI AHMED, *Campaigns and Response Executive,*
    late twenties
NICK WEBB, *Marketing and Communications Executive,*
    late twenties/early thirties
RYAN GIBSON, *intern, eighteen*
PAT WILLIAMS, *Humanitarian Manager, late fifties/*
    early sixties

Note on Text

/ indicates an interruption or quick response

– indicates where a sentence is stopped by the speaker

…indicates where a thought drifts away

Beat indicates a sudden change of tone

This text went to press before the end of rehearsals and so may differ slightly from the play as performed.

ACT ONE

Scene One

8.32 a.m. Christmas Eve.

The office of Disasters Relief, a small charity in London. Through the half-light, we can see it's a cramped, tatty room with four desks, grey metal filing cabinets with box files stacked on top, dying spider plants on shelves, dog-eared posters of refugees in tents during previous aid campaigns in Pakistan, Afghanistan and India, maps of north-east Asia, Africa, South America. There is also camping paraphernalia stacked in piles in various places. There's a dated TV. There's a door to Rory's office, a door to a stationery cupboard, and a door to a shared corridor and kitchen.

Last night was the Christmas party and the place is a bombsite – decorations hanging off the walls, snapped paper chains, tinsel, paper plates with bits of half-eaten sausage rolls. Chocolates have been trodden into the threadbare industrial carpet. Glasses with dregs of red wine, beer bottles and plastic cups are everywhere.

In the centre of a room is a two-man tent with the 'Disasters Relief' logo on the side. Around the tent are strewn shoes, a pair of trousers, tie, a bra, tights and socks.

The phone on PAT's *desk is ringing.*

ABI's *arm stretches out of the tent, feeling around for and grabbing a bra and T-shirt. She then emerges, hungover as hell, bleary-eyed, hair everywhere. She looks for which phone is ringing. It's confusing.*

She steps over the guy-ropes tied to desk legs and chairs, and just as she reaches it, it stops. The phone near NICK's *desk starts ringing. She looks for her clothes and picks up a skirt, lumberjack shirt and… realises. She looks around, realising, panicked.*

Enter NICK, *excited, carrying a cup of tea. He approaches* ABI.

NICK. Hey!

ABI. Hey.

NICK. You all right?

ABI (*half-laughs*). Fuck.

NICK. Yeah!

ABI. Fuck.

NICK. Yeah! Mental isn't it?

>   ABI *stares at* NICK, *taking in what's happened.*

Who woulda seen that coming! Office parties are supposed to be shit but that was… properly one of the best two or three parties *ever*!

>   NICK *follows* ABI's *gaze around.*

I know! You think this is bad, you ent seen the kitchen. It's like an epileptic's gone decorating.

Your head banging?!

It is isn't it?!

>   ABI *nods.*

Yeah, yeah mine's killing. Like badgers drilling inside it.

Here. Got ya a cup of tea, cup of camomile. I stuck four sugars in it and left the bag in. There's breakfast there. (*Points to a paper plate.*) Just a few crisps, sausage rolls, things. I took the hairs off. And one had a bite out of it but –

>   ABI *takes the plate.* NICK *puts the mug down. She looks to where the phone is ringing from.*

That's not helping is it? Been ringing all morning.

Giz a sec and I'll…

>   NICK *searches for the ringing phone. As he gets there, it stops ringing.*

Thank you!

ABI *puts the plate down and quickly picks up her clothes and begins putting them on.*

You know who I blame? That Chris Symonds from Food Aid. That moonshine of his yeah. Said he makes it out of courgettes. It's nuclear.

You remember doing his charity challenge?

ABI *smiles awkwardly, shaking her head.*

Abs, we were *ace*! You were downing it like water. One, bang. Two, bang. Fourteen! That bird from Age UK was destroyed!

And then us bustin' some moves, remember you on Pat's desk and getting Gordon Privett from Amnesty to give you the lift off *Dirty Dancing*.

ABI. I didn't?

NICK. You did! You must remember. He refused and so you lobbed a whole cheese at his head.

ABI (*laughs*). No!

NICK. You smacked him on his face. A whole brie. All melted, running down his cheeks! He's the Head of Regional Aid!

ABI. No! Fuck!

NICK. Yeah!

ABI (*grins*). I never did like him.

NICK. He knows that now!

NICK *rubs the fluff off a sausage roll and starts eating off the plate.*

Definitely the best party ever. You know what our new motto should be? 'Disasters Relief, we might be bust but we are The Best.'

Pringle?

Beat.

ABI. Wait, what's the time?

NICK. Half eight.

ABI. Half eight?

NICK. Yeah.

ABI. Then everyone'll be in. In like ten minutes.

NICK. No, s'all right, Abs /

ABI. Oh no no no /

NICK. Honestly /

ABI. Pat's normally in by eight, she'll be here any minute.

Nick, we've got to clear up and get –

NICK. It's Christmas Eve, Abs.

The office is closed. No one's in till the twenty-seventh.

ABI. – ?

NICK. It's just us. No Pat, no Rory, no work experience.

The place is ours. We can chill out. Or carry on where we left off.

I can't promise a repeat of last night but there is some magic left in the old wand.

NICK *goes in to touch* ABI *but she pulls back.*

ABI. So we did – ?

NICK. The Rude? Abi, mate, I'm not easily shocked like but I'm feeling violated, yeah. Some of last night was borderline illegal.

ABI. But we did use / ?

NICK. Toys?

ABI. Protection.

NICK. I'm pretty sure we used Old Reliable.

ABI. – ?

NICK. He's been tucked in my wallet for emergencies. One of them fruit ribbed ones. From a toilet. At uni.

ABI. Uni? How long ago was that?

NICK. 2003 weren't that long ago.

ABI. I gotta see it.

NICK. It's Old Reliable.

ABI. Nick, it's ten years old. You might as well've been wearing a hair net. Where is it?

NICK. Erm, dunno. Bin? Probably.

ABI. What we have done?

NICK. It was mainly missionary but /

ABI looks up.

Look, Abs, if the worst comes to the worst, I'll stand by you yeah, I'll do the right thing. Settle down in Luton, get a house and that. Whatever it takes.

ABI has finished getting dressed.

ABI. We should get that down. Cleaners could still be coming in.

NICK begins untying the guy-ropes tied to the desk legs. She pulls out NICK's remaining sock and throws it to him. She takes the sleeping mats out and rolls them up.

NICK. Oh yeah. Clear the crime scene.

Not that it was a crime. Unless the moonshine had Rohypnol.

Not that I put –

ABI. Nick?

NICK. I'm shutting up. I'm gonna stop talking.

This is all kind of

Weird…

As they dismantle the tent, ABI lifts one end and NICK lifts the other. ABI waits and NICK moves to her. Which way to turn the folded tent? They try one way, fail, then the next before settling on the first way. They fold it again.

…nice weird. I'm just, I suppose, I didn't think this would ever

Happen.

I thought there might something, like that time we did the Bangkok floods, in the camp there was… flirting. That was the first time I thought, maybe

And ever since I've felt… and so this is proper

It's kind of dream shit.

ABI. Is it?

NICK. Yeah. Best Christmas present I coulda got, Abs.

ABI. Nick? You're my best mate and you're lovely and it would be lovely but –

ABI *holds up her left hand to show the engagement ring on her finger, looking shamed.*

Bangkok was two years ago.

The wedding's in May. It's all paid for.

NICK. –

ABI. Sorry.

NICK. Yeah cool yeah. Completely cool. No issues.

I mean we work together. Be a nightmare.

Batman and Robin never… And Band Aid would never have happened, if Geldof and Midge Ure had…

ABI. Is that – ?

NICK. Yeah! Yeah! We're both adults. It's the twenty-first century isn't it. Just cos we've… doesn't mean it has to be a big deal.

And it's not like, individually, we've never had a one-night stand before.

ABI. I haven't. I've never cheated on Jaz or anyone. I'm not that sort of person. Last night's the first time I've ever done anything like that. Ever.

I'm such a muppet.

NICK. No! You're not, Abs. You're ace.

And anyway I wouldn't blame you. Cos he's –

ABI. What?

NICK. Nah, nah, nothing. It's none of my business.

ABI. Nick?

NICK. See, thing is... you're wicked. But when he's around...
   when we're in the pub on Fridays and he comes along.

ABI. Jaz likes coming out.

NICK. That's it, Abs. Does he? Cos whenever I speak to him,
   he ent the friendliest.

ABI. Being an underwriter is dead stressful.

NICK. Yeah, but so stressful that he has to be totally
   patronising, talking to us like we're doing some sort of
   worthy hobby.

ABI. That's just your perception.

NICK. And like when he says all that shit to you. Cos seriously,
   Abs, when I hear what he says, like, having a massive go cos
   you shouldn't be drinking or you should cover yourself up / or

ABI. Don't go there.

NICK. It's not a brown thing.

ABI. He's not like that. You don't see the real Jaz. He's really
   kind underneath... sometimes he can be dead generous.

NICK. Look, I just know that if I –

ABI. Don't.

NICK. I won't say I reckon you deserve better.

   Just someone less bell-end-y.

   ABI*'s phone rings.*

ABI. That'll be him.

   NICK *finds the phone in the bottom of a sleeping bag. He
   shakes it out and passes the phone to* ABI.

   It's Pat.

NICK. Why's she calling? Don't answer it. She'll be trying to get you into work.

ABI *gestures sarcastically 'I'm sort of at work'.* ABI *looks at the phone and goes to answer.*

It's Christmas. We're on annual leave.

ABI *looks to* NICK, *undecided, until the phone rings out.* NICK *finds his bag.* ABI *then opens up a text message on the phone.* ABI *sits at her desk, puts her hand over her mouth.* NICK *doesn't notice immediately, but then…*

Abs?

ABI. About a hundred missed calls. From Jaz.

ABI *scrolls through the text messages.*

(*Mumbles.*) Oh nonononono /

Did you see anyone with this last night?

NICK. Er, no.

ABI *scrolls through the texts.*

ABI. Someone's texted him back.

Oh my God.

'She's too good for you. Bell end'

NICK *looks incredibly sheepish.*

Why would you do this?

There's a text from him.

'Chat needed'

ABI *looks up to* NICK.

So what was it?

For a laugh?

NICK. We were all mucking about on our phones so, we were pissed and maybe I was trying to… save you from a life of

ABI. Save me from a life of happiness and security?

NICK. But you're not like him, you're smart and funny and full of... unbelievable, you save people's lives and he's just a stuck-up –

ABI. Look, you can't just interfere in someone else's life. It's not right.

NICK. I know but –

He is a twat.

ABI. No, no, Nick, you are a twat. A massive one.

Closely followed by me for letting last night happen.

ABI *puts on her coat.*

NICK. Wai-wait, Abs, listen.

ABI. Er no, Nick. I'm going home now to stop the person who I love, Nick, the person I *love*, leaving me.

Turn off the lights and do the code for the door.

ABI *picks up her bag and makes to exit.*

NICK. But it was for the best, Abs.

ABI. If you want to do something 'for the best', Nick, I suggest you try sticking your big sweaty head up your fat furry arse.

Enter RYAN, *dressed in coat, scarf and hat and covered with a dusting of snow. He's really anxious and flustered.*

RYAN. I'm really sorry I'm late.

RYAN *enters and begins taking off his outdoor clothes and setting himself up at his desk.*

There was something wrong with the Circle Line. A signal failure at Edgware Road or something. Probably the snow. But I tried really hard to get here as soon as I could but the buses weren't going past Angel so I had to walk and I got lost and my phone needs charging and

ABI. Ryan, what are you doing?

RYAN. I'll make up the time and stay late.

> Pat isn't [here]? You won't tell Pat or Rory cos I haven't been late at all and I don't want to let you down. Especially as this is such an amazing opportunity. And to have Disasters Relief on my CV it really means… it really will be so good for me /

ABI. Ryan, it's Christmas Eve.

NICK. You don't have to be in.

RYAN. Yes but /

NICK. Day after the Christmas party, mate.

> And even if the office was open

> You're the work experience

RYAN. Intern actually.

NICK (*quick*). Same thing?

RYAN. No, it's actually different

NICK. Is it?

RYAN (*quicker*). Work experience is what you do at school and being an intern /

NICK. Is getting experience of work

RYAN. Yeah but /

NICK. Which is totally different from work experience.

ABI. Nick!

RYAN (*really flustered now*). Anyway Pat said.

NICK. Pat?

RYAN. She said come in as soon as you can.

> She didn't call you?

NICK. Erm.

RYAN. You don't know?

> You haven't seen the news?

> Have you not heard what's happened?

Scene Two

8.50 a.m. Christmas Eve.

NICK, ABI *and* RYAN *look up at the TV screen in the corner of the office. BBC News 24.*

We see the sight of buildings collapsed, piles of rubble, children's faces covered in dust, makeshift tents, people searching through piles of concrete. On the rolling banner reads: 'PAKISTAN EARTHQUAKE: 7.4 RICHTER SCALE'.

NICK *holds his iPhone in his hand and concurrently checks Twitter.*

RYAN. It was seven point four on the Richter scale. The epicentre was ten miles south of Muzaffarabad. They're saying one thousand are missing.

ABI. But that'll shoot up. Seventy-five thousand died in 2005. At least. And the rebuilding work's not finished from last time.

This could be like proper bad.

NICK. Double whammy. What are the chances of –

Kashmir. Same place.

ABI *pulls up the Foreign Office website on her PC. She listens to a voice message on her phone.*

What are we gonna do?

RYAN. Pat said to wait till she gets in. Then we'll work out how we're going to respond.

NICK. My mate Sonal's family live near there. She lost everything last time. Husband, two of her kids, most of her farm.

What time's Pat getting here?

ABI *(indicates phone)*. Says she's stuck on a train.

RYAN (*shrugs*). The snow is particularly heavy across Kent and Surrey.

NICK. Brilliant. And what about our other great leader?

ABI. Rory's in his 'darling' little cottage in Devon remember.

NICK. Great.

ABI. We've got to clear up before Pat gets here.

NICK. We can't clean up all this, it's trashed. It'll take hours.

ABI *pulls apart some black bin liners and passes them around.*

ABI. People are kind of dying, Nick. We need to make a response.

ABI *holds out a bin liner to* NICK.

Unless you'd prefer responding by text?

NICK *reluctantly takes the bin liner. They begin picking up plates of half-eaten pizza slices, crisps, soaked party streamers, bits of cakes, etc. As they begin picking rubbish up,* RYAN *looks between* NICK *and* ABI, *trying to work out what's going on.*

RYAN. It was such an awesome party. When I was applying, like sending the letters out for internships, people said 'you don't wanna work in charity' cos everyone's like bit kind of… stiff, you know, but you, everyone, you're not, no way, not after –

That was in a very real sense – carnage.

ABI. You don't know how right you are.

NICK *picks up a crushed can of Coke.*

NICK. Look at this. Crushed.

ABI *points to a pile of disgusting mushed-up food.*

ABI. Look at this. Limp.

NICK *drops a plate of leftovers into his bag.*

NICK. So funny.

I can't do this.

NICK *hands his bin liner to* RYAN *and slumps into a seat and plays with this iPhone.*

ABI. Nick, I can't do it myself.

NICK. You're the Response Manager. Responding.

ABI. Nick, don't make me play the serious woman. I feel like I'm in an advert for Jif.

NICK. Maybe we should put a red line down the room and see who finishes first.

RYAN. I really don't mind doing it all. If you have work to do.

ABI (*to* NICK). At least turn your PC on. Unless you've got an app that clears up earthquakes?

NICK. I'm checking Twitter. As communications is my job.

ABI. We'll need to have something on the website before lunch. Which is four hours.

NICK *ostentatiously turns the PC on.* ABI *finds a photocopy of someone's bum and testicles. The PC makes the Windows start-up jingle.* NICK *takes a five-pound note from his pocket.*

NICK (*to* RYAN). Ryan mate, leave the clearing, come here, come here.

RYAN *looks to* ABI. *He then approaches* NICK.

Can you do us a favour and get us a Coke from the shop?

And Berocca.

RYAN *nods enthusiastically.* NICK *takes a ten-pound note from his pocket.*

And Nurofen for Abs.

He gives the ten pounds to RYAN *and takes the five-pound note back.*

RYAN. And your Salt and Vinegar Mini Cheddars?

NICK. That would be lovely. Cheers, lad.

Anything else you want, Abs?

ABI *shakes her head. Exit* RYAN. ABI *has filled a bin liner.*

Cute isn't he? I remember being eighteen. Wide-eyed, full of hope, a life solely dedicated to wanking.

ABI. Really, you: a wanker?

NICK *picks up his bin liner and continues dropping stuff in it.* ABI *ties the bin liner.*

NICK. Look, Abs, can we just

Talk – ?

ABI. About what – ?

NICK. You know!

ABI. I don't think there's much to say. I have to call Jaz so –

NICK. I just wanna –

Last night you said –

ABI. Nick, last night didn't happen.

Let's concentrate on doing our jobs. As professionals, yeah?

NICK. But –

ABI. End of story.

Exit ABI*, carrying a full bin liner, preparing to dial on her phone.*

NICK *is a bit lost. He drops another piece of rubbish off his desk. Then pulls his desk drawer out, tips it up and empties what looks like sick into the bin liner.*

Enter PAT*, dressed in padded coat, woollen hat and gloves. She looks over the mess, disgusted, while taking off her coat.* NICK *turns and sees her.*

PAT. You're in.

NICK. Yeah.

PAT. You didn't pick up my calls. I was ringing non-stop.

NICK. Oh sorry yeah, it's been all hands to the deck here. Bad journey? Sounds like you had / a

PAT. You wouldn't believe it. Three hours to go a twenty-seven-minute journey. I told them at the ticket office I wanted a full refund. You know what the man said? First of all he gave me that look, you know that stoned look where they don't blink. Then he said there was nothing he could do because it was an Act of God. I said earthquakes are an Act of God. Tidal waves are an Act of God. A snowfall is an annual seasonal occurrence. Which they should be prepared for. It's a disgrace. Isn't it, isn't it a disgrace?

NICK. Did he say their inability to cope was down to the heart of the railway being ripped out by privatisation resulting in a poorly maintained system which values the profits of shareholders over investment and has a wilful disregard for the welfare of passengers?

PAT. No.

NICK. Thought not.

PAT. He gave me a complaint form.

I asked him if he was aware what had happened in Pakistan. And if he knew how important what I had to do was. He didn't.

My gloves are wet.

Have we had any word from Rory yet?

NICK. His email said he'd left Devon. Three hours ago.

PAT. So he's still on the road then?

NICK. Unless he's in his batmobile.

PAT. Is he in a batmobile?

NICK. No.

PAT. So what have you done so far?

NICK. Concentrating on the clear-up, mainly.

PAT. Clear-up?

NICK. The devastation. We thought that was the priority.

Enter ABI, *holding a dustpan and brush and her phone*.

PAT. Do we know what the scale was? How big an area was affected?

NICK. It was mainly in here.

Complete carnage.

Rory's chair's broken. Abi's desk's a tip and I've just found a small mound of sick in my drawer.

PAT *stares at* NICK, *after realising*.

In here. Not Pakistan.

PAT (*tuts*). Have you done anything else?

NICK. My computer's on.

ABI. We were waiting for you to get here.

PAT. Me? Why?

ABI. You said to wait?

PAT. I didn't.

ABI. You did. On the phone to Ryan / ?

PAT. Who's Ryan?

NICK. New intern. Sits in Brian's chair. Looks like a bouffant hobbit.

PAT. I said for *him* to wait, not you. This is why I was calling. I can't believe you haven't done anything.

NICK *presents the room*.

But on the assessment.

ABI. No because you /

PAT (*sighs*). Let's get out of second gear then? Honestly, you need your hands held all the time. There are children in Malawi who walk ten miles a day for water and you can't even turn all the lights on.

PAT *turns on the remaining light and looks to the TV.*

What do we know? What's the latest?

ABI. Just what's on the news. BBC and Sky are saying there's a thousand missing.

NICK. At the moment.

ABI. Yeah, at the moment.

NICK. But that'll go up. Inevitably.

ABI *fixes* NICK *with a 'butt out' kind of stare.*

ABI. We know the epicentre was near Muzaffarabad in Kashmir.

PAT. And?

ABI. That's about it.

PAT. How big an area is affected? Do we know how many homes were destroyed?

ABI. There's not much, in terms of facts. At the moment.

PAT. Nothing?

NICK. Cos we're both shaken. What's happened here's really affected us. And we're trying to work out where we stand.

ABI. No, I think we know exactly where we stand.

PAT (*to* NICK). We have to do our jobs. Obviously.

ABI. Exactly.

PAT. What's the UN saying?

ABI. They don't know any more than we do.

PAT. So you've done nothing and you know nothing. It's like working with the Coalition. Let's get working on basic facts at least. Have you done the FAQs, Nick?

NICK. Not quite.

ABI. You haven't started the Frequently Asked Questions, Nick? It's normally your job.

NICK. Thank you, Abi.

PAT. You haven't even started it?

NICK. I am on it from this second onwards.

PAT. No, you look – (*Disapproving look*.) Abi, you do the
FAQs. And get the free boy to help.

Come on, we need to get moving. The people of Pakistan are
going to be sick, injured and looking to us for shelter. We do
tents best remember.

Abi, what about everyone else? What's Oxfam doing?

ABI. No word as yet.

PAT. CAFOD? The rest of the universe?

ABI *shakes her head and flicks through the web.*

ABI. No. (*Points to her screen*.) Merlin, Christian Aid,
WaterAid: they're all waiting for the DEC.

PAT. Good. Then we'll be first.

ABI. First?

PAT. Rory wants us… he wants to have our tents in villages by
Boxing Day.

ABI. But that's –

NICK (*counts*). Eight working hours.

ABI. And we can't… Pat, we need to assess… I mean, it's
like… we don't know the damage, the casualties, the needs,
the resources, anything. It's a week for assessment, then four
days' procurement, a week minimum for distribution /

PAT. That's not the way –

ABI. We can't supply what we don't know.

PAT. If this earthquake's in the same place as 2005, with the same
damage, same injuries and the same need, what we'll do /

NICK. Is the same response?

PAT. Well done, very good. Shelagh and the board say we can
use the emergency funds from the flood appeal. There's
twenty-six thousand pounds in there.

ABI. So we're partnering Oxfam again?

PAT. No. Rory wants us acting independently.

ABI. But we've never done that.

PAT. It's all about speed, Abi. If we're out first. And be recognised for it – maybe the funders will start to come back.

You know how dire our situation is.

ABI. How dire? Exactly?

PAT. I told you last night.

ABI. Did you?

NICK. We haven't won a grant for six months. The barrel's run dry.

PAT. Shelagh wants us shut down, the board want us shut down. But it won't happen, I've told them.

NICK. Fight the power, Patricia.

PAT. Yes I am, Nick. This is important.

Now, it looks like a category four. Abi, contact the tent man in Pakistan.

NICK. Khalid Bhatt? He's your favourite, Abs. The Millets of Muzaffarabad.

PAT. And tell him how many tents we need and get a sense of cost – tell him he must get them sourced and delivered by the twenty-sixth.

ABI. Pat, I really think we should stick to process?

PAT. Nick, I want an appeal portal on the website by lunch.

NICK. On it like a car bonnet.

ABI. Pat, due process –

PAT. Then FAQs, stats, charts and a proposal for the board by two. It all starts now. This is it, the big push. I want us all completely focused.

Is that tea?

NICK. Coffee.

PAT. I'm going to get a tea.

    PAT *exits before hearing any answer.*

ABI. Fuck.

NICK. Language.

Scene Three

10.47 a.m. Christmas Eve.

The office space is now cleared. ABI *and* RYAN *are on their phones. Dialling, listening, hanging up. Dialling, listening, hanging up.* NICK *works on the website. He drinks from a glass of Berocca.*

There's now a large map of Pakistan/India on the wall with a red spot where the epicentre was and the perimeter of the affected area marked in thick red pen.

ABI. Anything, Ryan?

    RYAN *shakes his head.*

RYAN. It's ringing out.

ABI. Keep trying. And get other numbers from the website.

    They'll be people who know him.

    There's contacts on the shared drive.

    (*Puts a folder on his desk.*) And look for numbers in this. Try everyone.

    ABI *returns to her desk and begins trying to call. As she waits for a reply, she checks her mobile phone for a message from Jaz.*

    Has this [phone] rung?

NICK. Nope.

Enter PAT *with urgency from Rory's office, landline phone in her hand, and looks at the TV.*

PAT (*to phone*). I'm watching the TV now, Rory.

(*To* NICK.) What's the latest?

NICK. Up to three thousand dead.

PAT. Tsk.

(*To phone*.) Three thousand.

(*To* NICK.) Has Cameron spoken?

NICK. No, his fag ent woken him up yet.

PAT. Has he?

NICK. No.

PAT *indicates that* NICK *should turn the sound on with the zapper.* NICK *tries but it doesn't work. He stands next to the TV and presses the 'mute' button to unmute it.* ABI *begins calling Jaz.*

PAT. Obama?

NICK. Nope. Or Nick Clegg so –

PAT (*to phone*). No one as yet, Rory. But we'll let you know.

PAT *hangs up.*

(*To* NICK.) The A35's at a standstill. He's stuck in a snow drift near Dorchester.

PAT *checks her watch.*

The BBC do disasters well don't they? I've always thought they come into their own with a disaster. Princess Diana was handled wonderfully. And the Japanese tsunami. They really rise to the occasion.

He's very handsome isn't he? She had cancer but I don't like her. He is handsome.

Have you been drinking vinegar?

NICK. No.

PAT. Is that a school? Goodness.

> PAT *puts her hand over her mouth.* PAT *goes to her desk and hangs up. Without sitting, she begins scrolling through her emails on screen. Concurrently,* ABI *leaves a quiet voice message for Jaz.*

ABI. Hi Jaz, it's me again. I'm not gonna leave here for hours so. Listen whatever you're thinking, honestly it really isn't what you think. It's all fine. Call me back soon, yeah?

> ABI *hangs up. And then tries to call her contact.*

PAT. If there is a silver lining to this story then it's the timing. Christmas is actually a very good time to have a disaster. It's the season of good will. The milk of human kindness is very fresh. People are a lot more relaxed about putting their hands in their pockets.

> Look at the tsunami. Not the Japanese one. The one before. The Indonesians did very well to have their tsunami on Boxing Day.

> It was good timing.

NICK. If there ever is a good time to lose one hundred and sixty-seven thousand people.

PAT. You know what I mean.

> We wouldn't have raised fourteen billion if it wasn't /

NICK. It wasn't just us.

PAT. No but we helped.

> And that's something to remember in funding applications.

NICK. There's no chance we'll get the same donations again.

> PAT *looks up, annoyed.*

> Pakistan ent exactly Haiti in PR terms.

> They had the last earthquake, the floods – twice. Then there's Al-Qaeda, corruption, bombings, terrorism, cricket-match fixing. People might be a bit –

PAT. Let's not second guess the public, Nick. They're not all as prejudiced.

NICK. I'm not saying /

    PAT *checks her watch.*

PAT. You've got the FAQs?

NICK. That was Abi.

    ABI *then points to* RYAN.

PAT (*to* RYAN). FAQs?

RYAN. Er, yeah. Here.

    RYAN *panics and rummages at speed through the piles of paper on his desk to give the impatient* PAT *a piece of printed paper.*

NICK. And you looked at what's being said on Twitter, mate?

RYAN. Erm –

PAT. Come on, I need all the information you can find. We must know how many tents are needed and where.

RYAN (*scrolling on screen*). It's not like facts and stuff. It's just people, like, people like, you know, sort of saying stuff.

NICK. Whatever you've got, fella.

RYAN. It's not –

    They are all looking at RYAN.

    Er... Oh... if you're sure?

    Okay.

    'This is what you get for hiding Bin Laden.'

    'Christmas has come early. Thank you Santa.'

    'God 2, The Pakis Nil.'

    'Shame it didn't happen in Bradford.'

    NICK *winces.* PAT *stares at* RYAN.

PAT. Very disappointing.

RYAN. I don't think that!

PAT. You know Abi's family's from Bradford.

RYAN. But I don't think –

PAT. No, you didn't.

> PAT *takes the paper from* RYAN.

> If you manage to find anything useful, I want to know. I'm using Rory's office today so if you need me –

> *Exit* PAT *to Rory's office.* NICK *finishes working on the website.* ABI *slams her phone down, annoyed.*

ABI. Buggerbuggerbugger.

> Anything, Ryan?

RYAN. I've tried all the numbers and there's… it's like a dead tone now.

ABI. You've tried Sulaman Patel?

RYAN. Yeah.

NICK. What's up?

ABI. We can't get through to Khalid Bhatt.

> NICK *switches his attention away from his PC and to* ABI.

NICK. At all?

ABI. Ryan's tried his office, mobile, text.

NICK. What about PakRes?

ABI. I've just tried.

NICK. And?

> ABI *shakes her head.*

> Where's his office?

ABI. Rawalpindi.

NICK. Edge of the zone. (*Points on map.*) Power lines must be down. They'll be up again soon.

ABI (*to* RYAN). Keep trying.

> RYAN *keeps dialling, listening, hanging up, dialling, listening, etc.*

> Damn. (*Looks at the clock.*)

NICK. Wai-wait, Abs. Wasn't he… after the last earthquake, didn't he move? I could swear he shifted his office to –

> NICK *points on the map to a spot inside the affected zone.*

ABI. Oh. Yeah.

NICK. Challa Bandi.

ABI. Shit.

NICK. S'all right is Khalid.

> ABI *points towards a photo of her and Khalid giving out tents during the previous earthquake.*

RYAN. Where's that?

ABI. The last earthquake. He's always grinning like that. He's the best supply man I've ever worked with. He got us two thousand tents in two days.

NICK. Total lege.

ABI. Poor bloke.

NICK. Don't worry, Abs. He'll be all right. The network'll be down, or the phone lines, you know. Few hours, a day or two, the power will be up. We'll get a better idea then.

ABI. We haven't got a few days, Nick. We need tents now.

NICK. Then you'll have to tell Pat the launch will take longer.

ABI. Er… no.

NICK. Er, why not?

ABI. She'll stare at me, do the grin – (*A rictus grin.*) and then completely flip. The last thing we need is Pat running round like Gazza on crack.

NICK. Got to be done though.

ABI. Maybe *you* should then?

NICK. Your contact.

ABI. And you're the comms man.

NICK. Yeah but *I'm* not to blame for losing our only supplier in Kashmir.

ABI. How am I to – ?

NICK. Your job to call him.

ABI. Only because you're too hungover.

NICK. That's not my fault.

ABI. Erm??

> NICK *makes a 'What, me?' gesture.*

What is it about blokes that you glory in hangovers like it's a personal achievement? My brother's like that when he's had a really big shit.

NICK. Look, *I* know you ent to blame. I'm just saying it as she'll see it.

ABI. Exactly! And that's why I'm not telling her. *You* are doing it.

NICK. Er, yeah, but I kind of value my love-plums.

> PAT *enters towards her desk, unseen by* ABI *or* NICK. *She picks up a folder from her desk.*

ABI. Of course, it's where your thinking gets done.

NICK. I'm not telling Pat.

> PAT *stops.*

PAT. Tell Pat, what?

ABI. Nothing.

> NICK *looks at* ABI *then to* PAT.

NICK. Cup of tea?

Scene Four

11.10 a.m. Christmas Eve.

ABI *scowls at* NICK. *She has her desk-phone receiver pressed to her ear, waiting for an answer.* NICK *is at his desk, flicking through his old Rolodex.* RYAN *works at his desk, occasionally making notes in a small notebook. He has a can of Fanta on his desk.*

ABI. Thanks a million, Nick. That was amazing.

NICK. I didn't have a choice –

ABI. No – ?

NICK. – /

ABI. Amazing. You are a-mazing. I really am seeing the real you today, aren't I?

NICK. But what was I going to –?

ABI. You could have at least built up to it. Break the news gently.

Instead of spilling your guts.

(*On connection to answerphone, breezily.*) Hi Claire, it's Abi Ahmed at Disasters Relief. We met at the EPAK seminar in October. We're looking for tent suppliers in Pakistan. If you could call me back today, I'd be really grateful.

Concurrently, NICK *flicks through his contacts and finds a card. He starts dialling on the landline and holds the receiver in the crook of his neck, watching* ABI.

NICK. Mate, we've only got five hours. She needed telling.

ABI. And now she's panicking. So we're all panicking.

The last thing we need is us –

NICK. What?

ABI. Point-scoring.

NICK. Who's point-scoring?

ABI. You're not?

NICK. As long as you're not.

ABI. So that little confession just now?

NICK. She'd have found out some time.

ABI. So you got the first shot in. Like always. Interfering.

NICK. No!

ABI. Rubbish! Trying to be golden-bollocks. You're so obvious, Nick. I've seen windows less transparent.

NICK *makes a call on his phone and holds his hand up for* ABI *to stop speaking*.

NICK. All right, Irfan mate. Yeah, erm, it's Nick Webb for Disasters here. Abi's lost our snout in Kashmir so wondered if you've got any contacts spare? It's kind of urgent if you can call us back that would be… sweet. Nice one, mate. Cheers.

NICK *puts the receiver down but in the meantime* ABI *has made a call*.

Look, Abs, we should / at least – ?

ABI. Hi Bastian, it's Abi from Disasters Relief. We're looking for anyone who can supply tents, shelters, bedding. Please call me back here or on my mobile, thanksbye.

ABI *hangs up*.

NICK. Abs, all I want is this campaign launched, to go home and eat my own bodyweight in mince pies. That's it.

ABI. Good.

NICK. No mucking about.

ABI. Because she's going to be looking for mistakes.

NICK. I know.

ABI. Someone to sack if all goes tits up.

NICK. Thanks, I do remember what happened to Brian –
(*Points to* RYAN*'s desk*.) God rest his soul.

ABI. Exactly.

NICK. So I'm giving this one hundred and ten per cent, Abs, no
distractions. There are gonna be a million people over there,
freezing, who need shelter. They're the only ones I'm
concentrating on.

ABI. Really? So you're not at all looking out for yourself?

NICK. Nope.

ABI. All this good work you're doing, it's completely selfless.
Helping others, taking no credit, feeling their pain.

NICK. Yep.

ABI. Because you're such a good, virtuous person.

NICK. Again yep.

RYAN *starts paying attention to* NICK *and* ABI*'s
conversation.*

ABI. I'm not sure the evidence supports you, Nicholas.

NICK. Er, I think it does. Four years I've been here. Two years
at WaterAid. Before that, a year volunteering at the DEC.
I've done chugging on the streets, three 10-K runs – all
sponsored for Parkinsons – and I have a standing order for
Amnesty.

ABI. Stunning.

NICK. And no offence but that slightly trumps wearing hemp
shoes and using Ecover washing-up liquid.

ABI. That's totally unfair. I volunteered for a year in Ghana, off
my own back, I help out at my hospice in Hendon, I'm doing
a half marathon in June – for infant cancer – and I've got a
direct debit for Greenpeace.

NICK. How much for?

ABI. Ten pounds a month.

NICK. Fifteen for Amnesty.

> NICK *looks to* RYAN *for approval.*

ABI. Well done you. Not all of us are moneyed.

NICK. Meaning what please?

ABI. Perhaps my giving comes from here – (*Heart.*)

NICK. So you're, what, more genuine?

ABI. Being working class means I'm down to earth, unpretentious.

NICK. Working class! How are you working class?

ABI. Because I say class – (*To rhyme with lass.*)

NICK. That doesn't make you working class.

ABI. In my house it does.

NICK. You live in Crouch End. You read the *Guardian* and eat Dorset Cereal.

ABI. I was talking about my family.

NICK. Which is where please?

ABI. Bradford, as you know.

NICK. Where your dad is a – ?

ABI. Doctor. So?

NICK. And you have a five-bedroom house.

ABI. It's not the stuck-up home counties.

NICK. Being born north of Watford doesn't make you 'real'.

ABI. But more real than growing up in a soulless commuter town.

NICK. Reading is not soulless. It's got the Oracle shopping centre and excellent access to the M4.

ABI. I rest my case.

NICK. What's not genuinely good about me then?

ABI. Well, that's been workshopped already today.

But this, cheeky-chappy Jamie Oliver thing. This 'all right geezer, giz a butcher's at yer apples 'n' pears' is genuine, Nick?

NICK. Yeah.

ABI. And this lumberjack-shirt thing, that's your natural look is it, reflecting your heritage… lumbering.

NICK. It's just a shirt.

ABI. A carefully chosen shirt.

NICK. It was the only clean one I had. Yesterday.

ABI. And the carefully ruffled hair.

NICK. Er, I don't really get what you're trying to say.

Am I not genuine?

ABI. Okay, answer me this, Nicholas. Are you honestly in it because you want to genuinely help people?

NICK. Yes.

ABI. And not because you love having an interfere. Helping 'poor little brown people' live just like you.

NICK. No! I'm totally straight up.

ABI. Totally.

NICK. As far as anyone is concerned I am Mother fucking Teresa.

ABI looks at him as if he's an idiot. NICK grins. NICK checks his computer screen. ABI's mobile phone rings.

ABI. Jaz?

Oh. Hi there, Bastian – (*Look to* NICK.) thanks for calling back. How are you? (*Short reply.*) So well, thank you. (*Short reply.*) No, I'm not asking for a date but thank you. (*Short reply. Laughs, flirting.*) It's something a bit different. Give me a moment.

Exit ABI.

NICK. Fun this isn't it?

RYAN. – ?

NICK. It's not like this all the time. Mostly we're all very calm, civilised.

RYAN. Yeah. Kind of intense, ha.

NICK *looks after where* ABI *has gone*.

Do you… I mean… like, you and Abi, are you always – ?

It's kind of like you hate each other.

NICK. All that [arguing]? No, that's just… it's banter really.

She's wicked, Abi. It probably sounds like… but, it's all kind of joking.

Isn't it?

RYAN. If you say so.

NICK. There's no problem, at all. We're cool, nothing's [happened]. Normal diplomatic relations are in place.

RYAN *nods sagely*.

RYAN. Hmm!

NICK. What? Why are you looking all 'knowing'?

RYAN. I don't have an opinion. I'm just the work experience.

NICK. Exactly.

RYAN. I know nothing. Except that you were wearing that shirt yesterday.

NICK. Yeah, and? So what? What are you… the fashion police?

RYAN. And you were both here when I got in this morning.

And knew nothing about the earthquake.

NICK. Whoa whoa, back up there, big fella.

Whatever you're thinking, whatever you suspect, yeah, it's wrong so, you know, you can keep your, whatever theories to yourself, don't say anything.

RYAN *looks knowingly again*.

RYAN. You're not properly in to her then?

NICK. You what! No! No!

RYAN. You're 'just good friends'.

NICK. Look, I'm not in love with Abi, all right.

On hearing 'love', RYAN's eyebrows shoot through the roof.
NICK *notices.*

Listen, you have to watch what you say in here. Use the
wrong words and it can get you in proper trouble.

RYAN. I don't get what you [mean]?

NICK. Like you before yeah, saying Paki. Whoa.

RYAN. Me?

NICK. In that tweet.

RYAN. That wasn't –

NICK. Even so, sensitivity to your workmates – (*Points to*
ABI*'s desk.*)

RYAN. I didn't mean – !

NICK. I know. But Abi might not. And Pat, she doesn't have the
sharpest sense of humour. You don't wanna end up like Brian.

RYAN. Who sat here?

NICK. He was leading the response on the Syria appeal. Used
the C word.

RYAN. C–U–N–T?

NICK. Worse. Coloured.

RYAN. Oh.

NICK. He was out on his arse like that – (*Clicks fingers.*) We
had a complete shutdown while we checked all his emails for
C-bombs. We had a training day on language, new
guidelines, all that.

Take it from me, you really don't wanna experience a
training day.

RYAN. Does it not matter more what the intention is? Behind the word.

NICK. You would think so, wouldn't you.

RYAN. My granny says coloured and she's not –

NICK. A racist, course not!

RYAN. She says half-caste too.

My mum told her to say mixed race but she said it sounded like an Olympic event.

What about black. Is that all right here…?

NICK. In here, yeah. America though, definitely not.

RYAN. Why?

NICK. It's African-American always.

RYAN. In Australia, they say wog. My mate Kostas is from Brisbane. He says he's a wog. Everyone called him Woggy at school.

And he calls people Chinks. And Pakistanis are called Pakis there.

And Misha Nasciemento calls me nigger and I'm not even coloured.

NICK*'s landline phone rings. He answers it, moving away.*

NICK. Black.

RYAN. I know I / was joking.

NICK. Irfan mate! (*Reply.*) Yeah, you have? (*Reply.*) My man, you are an absolute beauty. You have literally saved… seriously, mate… I know you don't celebrate Christmas but I am gonna give you half of what… whatever you want: Big Trak, Scalextric, Xbox, anything.

Tell me more, mate.

NICK *grabs a piece of paper and pen and begins writing. Enter* ABI. *She goes to her desk and picks up a pen and finds a piece of paper.*

ABI (*to phone*). Honest, you're a godsend... lemme... give me his number again... Abdul Salim yep, yep... (*Scribbles her pen to get ink*.) sorry my pen's not... here we go... yep, yep. You're at Biggin Hill now? What time are you flying? Okay, hear from you when you get there. (*Reply*.) It would be lovely to see you too some time. (*Short reply*.) No, of course we won't. Bye, thanks *so much*. Bye.

    ABI *hangs up and looks at her phone happily, triumphant.* NICK*, hangs up.*

NICK (*to phone*). Cheers, geez.

    (*To* ABI.) All right?

ABI (*holding up the number*). Yeah, that was the lovely Bastian at Oxfam.

    NICK *mimes gagging.*

    I've got us a Pakistani partner.

NICK. Nice. So have I.

    NICK *holds up his piece of paper. The triumphant look on* ABI*'s face disappears.*

Scene Five

12.30 p.m. Christmas Eve.

The team is around PAT*'s desk in a team meeting.* RYAN *is standing on* PAT*'s chair/the furniture waving her mobile phone in the air at the highest point he can reach.*

PAT. Try again, higher.

There, higher.

(*Towards the phone.*) Is that better, Rory? Can you hear me now, Rory? Testing one two three?

ABI. Pat it's not going / to work cos

PAT. Sssh!

ABI. It's *his* phone with no reception.

PAT. Abi, quiet! I need to listen. Rory, say something if you can hear us.

NICK (*spooky voice*). Is anybody there?

PAT. Sssh! Rory?

RYAN *listens. Nothing.*

No? No. It's no good.

The one time we really need him and he's trapped in a Little Chef.

RYAN *climbs onto a filing cabinet. And stretches up.*

RYAN (*into phone*). Hello? Hi! Rory, you can hear us?

RYAN *gives a thumbs up.*

PAT. Can you stay there?

RYAN. Uh yeah.

PAT. Rory, you can listen in. You know Khalid's missing so we need to make a call on an alternative partner. So – ?

NICK *shoots his arm up like a schoolboy.*

Nick?

NICK. Sweet. Irfan Masri at Islamic Relief is over there now. He's got a bunch he's working with called Al-Qaram. He worked with them on the floods and says they're well run, well supplied and reliable.

PAT. Supplying what?

NICK. It's not exactly our thing.

ABI. So what?

NICK. We'd have to make an adjustment to our USP. But if you wanna move quick, get aid in there. They've got military helicopters stacked up to the roof ready to go.

PAT. With what?

NICK. Grain.

ABI. Grain?

NICK. I know it's not tents but people need grains for bread and stuff.

ABI. To make gingerbread houses?

NICK. Ooh, is that a rib gone?

ABI. Grain's only good if they can grind the corn. Are the windmills still standing?

NICK. Windmills? It's not medieval over there.

PAT. Do they want bread?

NICK. Who doesn't like bread?

RYAN. I don't like toast.

NICK. But – !

ABI. Some people might be wheat intolerant.

PAT. That is true. Will there be provision for gluten allergies?

NICK. You are having a giraffe.

PAT. I do get bloated sometimes. And after milk.

ABI. There will be people with IBS in Kashmir, Nick.

NICK. Wait!

ABI. Nick, we supply tents. Grain isn't tents.

NICK. Look, I know it ent perfect but do this and we can channel our cash into something people can get by tomorrow.

Donation. Supply. Delivery. All within twenty-four hours.

PAT. How will people know it's us? You can't brand grain can you?

ABI. Small pens?

NICK. Or on the sacking?

PAT. How big are the sacks? Can you see them in photographs?

NICK. Yeah but… forget the branding for a minute /

PAT. If they're small bags –

ABI. Or packets.

NICK. Okay but… for logos, I'd have to find a supplier, print or spray them, move them. It could take… days. Weeks maybe.

ABI. Time is of the essence.

NICK. But listen: go with this and we can splash photos, videos, everything all over the website. By Boxing Day. Imagine it, starving victims reaching up to our people handing down bags of grain. We'll get all the images from Irfan. Then we'll email all our donors and supporters with pictures, updates. Slave Labour can go all out on Facebook and Twitter and stuff.

What do you think?

PAT. Grain, Rory?

Rory?

RYAN *listens to the phone. Hears nothing. Shakes his head.*

NICK. Yes but –

Feeding people. Making a difference.

Quickly.

ABI *makes a playful 'dummy' face at* NICK.

PAT. Abi? What's yours?

ABI. Well, here's what I –

ABI *hands out pieces of a paper with a summary of the group.*

I don't really know –

They're quite new.

PAT. You said they're from a good source.

ABI. Oxfam.

They're called Green Crescent. They're based in Kashmir. Their director Abdul Salim approached Oxfam about supplying twenty thousand tents to fifteen villages in the isolated areas around Muzaffarabad.

NICK. *They* approached Oxfam?

ABI. Yeah. Is that an [issue] – ?

PAT. Tents. That does fit. And branded?

ABI. I don't know.

PAT. But you could, if you asked.

ABI. I can ask. We'll send templates.

PAT. I'll write that we can?

ABI. All you need is paint and a stencil.

NICK. Erm?

ABI. What?

PAT (*loud, for Rory*). Tents will go down well with the board.

NICK. And how much do we know about them?

ABI. As much as about yours?

NICK. Islamic Relief are English.

ABI. You've got a problem with Pakistanis?

NICK. No.

ABI. Brown people then?

NICK. No!

ABI. Just brown men?

PAT *looks at him, pointedly.*

NICK. What?!

I mean we can vouch for Islamic Relief at least.

Tent supplies could be just generous Boy Scouts. We can't take the risk, Pat.

PAT. If Oxfam can vouch for Green Crescent?

ABI. I'm sure.

NICK. Can they?

ABI. They go through due diligence before any money gets sent. Oxfam are very thorough. Bastian there said he likes them. Even if they are a 'bit foreign'.

NICK. Bastian Ridley. Jesus God.

PAT. What's wrong with Bastian? I like him. He's got lovely hair.

NICK. Abi, Bastian Ridley is an anus with a quiff.

PAT. Language!

ABI. Ooh, bit threatened by Bastian?

NICK. Am not.

ABI. He is all man. Six foot five is it?

PAT. He donates half his wages to a tribe in Peru.

NICK. What-ever! Please –

ABI. Anyway, he's spoken to them and says they're kosher.

NICK. Obviously not kosher.

ABI. You know what I mean.

NICK. He's definitely done due diligence on your Boy Scouts?

ABI (*betraying uncertainty*). Maybe.

NICK. And he's happy for us to steal his contact?

ABI. We're not stealing them. He pretty much said we could have them.

PAT. So Oxfam will vouch?

NICK. Sure? Cos I wouldn't be happy if you were stealing them.

ABI. He's giving them.

PAT. But if Abi's happy to vouch for Green Crescent?

We do need to get the campaign launched ASAP.

NICK. If you're not genuinely one hundred per cent confident in them.

Then we should go with my lot.

ABI. I am, yeah.

PAT. So you're vouching for them?

PAT *looks at* ABI.

Yes?

ABI. Yes.

NICK. Sure?

ABI. Yes.

PAT. We'll go with Green Crescent then? Yes?

Rory, yes? We'll take it as yes.

ABI *looks at* PAT, *then* NICK. PAT *turns to* ABI *and* NICK.

Very good. Well done, Abi.

Ask them what they need and how we can help.

Good, we're ready to launch.

Scene Six

1.38 p.m. Christmas Eve.

RYAN *sits at* NICK*'s desk with* NICK. ABI *enters with three mugs of tea and a cup of water. She puts the first mug on* RYAN*'s desk.*

ABI (*breezily*). Cuppa tea for you, er, loser.

> ABI *hands* NICK *his tea.*

NICK. Ha, that wasn't a loss.

ABI. No? Sort of looked like I… sort of, won?

NICK. Tactical loss.

ABI. Really?

NICK. Yeah yeah, long game and all that. You might have won the battle but, you know, my tanks are revving outside the Sudetenland.

ABI. Nice Nazi metaphor.

NICK. You know what I mean. Hadn't you better chase your Boy Scouts? You ent got long to commission them.

ABI. You know what, I might do that. And, er, single-handedly save the people of Pakistan and save our charity.

NICK. Yeah, well, I'm gonna –

ABI. Scratch your balls?

NICK. No.

ABI. Go on Facebook?

NICK. No.

ABI. Do your job? Promoting my work?

NICK*'s struck dumb. She smiles, victorious.* NICK *watches as* ABI *goes to her desk and puts her tea down before picking up the phone.*

RYAN. You like it?

NICK (*distracted by* ABI). Hmm?

RYAN (*pointing to the screen*). What I've done on the website?

NICK *goes to look at the screen.* RYAN *begins his demonstration.* NICK *is thinking more about* ABI.

This is the home page, I've moved the donation portal from there to there so it's the first thing you see. Click through and it suggests you donate twenty pound first so you have to specify less if you like.

NICK. Hmm.

ABI (*into phone*). Hello, my name is Abi Ahmed.

I'd like to speak to Mr Salim? We spoke before.

RYAN. There, there's a suggestion to direct debit. And examples of what your thirty pounds a month will buy. And link buttons to Facebook, Twitter and Reddit so people can share our site. I've tidied up the back-end so navigation is more intuitive. And added links to pages on Pakistan there, earthquake prevention and the charity commission.

NICK. And that's Green Crescent?

RYAN. As much as I can find. We can add more as we go. And use our contact database to inform subscribers of how they're doing.

NICK *looks over the website.*

ABI (*into phone*). Mr Salim, I need you to complete our forms on procurement, responsibility delegation and our approval and evaluation matrix. You'll need to fill them in online before we can authorise payment requisition. (*Reply.*) Yes, we'll need all forms completed by six p.m., GMT. Okay? (*Reply.*) I'll wait yes.

NICK. Mate, this is amazing.

RYAN. You like it?

NICK. You some kind of IT superman or something?

RYAN. It's quite simple, and sort of a hobby. I don't really 'do' friends so –

NICK. It's brilliant. I'm supposed to be Mr IT but I ent got a clue. I just cut and paste. This is wicked.

One thing you might want to do is stick a few more big images on there. Not the full Barnardos but you know… kids with flies, smashed dollies, that sort of thing.

RYAN. To grab people's attention.

NICK *looks over to* ABI.

NICK. You're learning, mate! We'll impress people with this.

RYAN. We will?

NICK. Oh yeah. You and me, geez. (*Points to* PAT*'s desk*.) She is gonna love it.

RYAN. Will you tell Pat that I did it?

NICK. Yeah, of course.

She might sign you up.

RYAN. Awesome!

Is there a job going?

NICK. Brian's maybe if you keep this up.

ABI (*into phone*). Yes, I will wait.

NICK. Good on ya, little fella.

I sort of feel like I wanna ruffle your hair. Can I ruffle your hair?

RYAN. Erm.

NICK *ruffles* RYAN*'s hair. Awkward*.

NICK. Think I need more Berocca.

Exit NICK.

ABI (*into phone*). You must tell me what you need by six p.m., okay? (*Reply.*) Yes, tents. Tents. (*Reply.*) Five hundred? (*Reply.*) No, not... (*Reply.*) Our budget is twenty-six thousand pounds. (*In English.*) Pounds sterling. Yes. Call me back when you have completed the matrix.

ABI *puts the phone down. She furiously scribbles on her notebook.*

RYAN. Is there anything I can help you with, Abi?

ABI. I need to send Mr Salim our suppliers' guide. He's emailing it back by six. Then I can get the money transfer set up and the paperwork done.

ABI *checks her mobile phone.*

Has this rung?

RYAN *shakes his head.*

RYAN. Jaz? He still hasn't called back?

ABI (*surprised at* RYAN*'s knowledge*). Hmm, no, nothing.

RYAN (*knowing*). Ah.

Is this because of what... last night?

ABI. You what?

How do you – ?

Did he – ?

RYAN *indicates 'yes'.*

RYAN. I was chatting with Nick and he sort of... said.

ABI. Said what?

RYAN. About...

ABI. You are kidding?

RYAN. It's all okay though. I mean that I don't think you need worry about anything. Because everything is cool.

ABI. Oh?

RYAN. No, because, if you're erm… if you're worried about Jaz… and think Nick might like get in the way, sort of between you… you don't need to worry cos he won't… Cos I asked Nick if he was like 'in to you' and he was like 'I'm not in love with Abi' so…

ABI. He's not.

RYAN. At all… so –

ABI*'s face falls*.

So it's all okay, isn't it?

You and Jaz are… (*Indicates 'okay'*.)

Beat.

I've said the wrong thing.

ABI. No. No. Not at all. Cos there's nothing –

RYAN. I have though haven't I? It's not what I meant. I wrote in my – (*Fetches notebook from desk*.) My old teacher Mrs Boxall said make notes, to learn. And she said one thing. 'Be like Magnolia paint. Clean, inoffensive and even if you're not exciting, everyone will want you.'

ABI. She sounds very wise, Mrs Boxall.

RYAN. I haven't been magnolia.

ABI. It's all right. Here's a note for your book. You can in no way trust him over there. He might be getting you to do all his web stuff. And he'll say your work's amazing and you're the greatest thing and you'll believe him but he won't mean it.

RYAN. So what he said about Brian's job…?

ABI. He said he'd get you that?

RYAN. See, I would like so completely love to work here. If there's a chance.

Mum says I should go to university but –

I don't see the point spending three years drinking and doing all those immature student things.

It probably is better to go into work.

ABI. Yeah?

RYAN. University's so expensive. How long did you take to pay off your student loan?

ABI. I still haven't. I've been scrimping for years and living off tuna pasta and I've only just finished saving for a deposit on a shoebox in Penge.

RYAN. With Jaz?

ABI. Five years to save thirty-five grand. I put fifteen in so –

RYAN. It's so depressing.

ABI. It's the way of the world, Ryan. Money's taken over and compromised everything. We're no different. We spend more time doing PR than actual aid on the ground.

RYAN. You see, that's why I want to work here. Because I really don't want to you know like be a total fascist. I think charity is the best way to change the world. I want to do whatever I can.

ABI. Work on the ground?

RYAN. Helping real people.

ABI. Not schmoozing and doing websites?

RYAN. Saving lives.

ABI. Then pull up a chair over here.

I'll get you started on the suppliers' procurement matrix. One thing you'll learn about charity is that we're incredible at paperwork.

RYAN. Should I not help Nick with the website?

ABI. What do you want to do with your life, Ryan?

RYAN. I want to make a difference.

ABI (*pulls up a chair by her desk*). Then have a seat, Mr Magnolia.

Scene Seven

7.46 p.m. Christmas Eve.

NICK *wears a Santa hat. He holds the office advent calendar in his hands, opening the remaining doors and eating the chocolates and sharing them with* RYAN.

ABI *is at the window of Rory's office, watching* PAT, *who is on the phone.*

NICK. How long is she gonna be on the phone for?

ABI. We're up to twenty-seven minutes. Don't think she's got a word in yet.

NICK. What's she talking about? All Shelagh has to say is 'We approve the campaign' and we're launched.

ABI. It is Shelagh, remember. She'll being picking holes in every detail.

NICK. You gotta wonder who runs this place. Is it not a bit mental that there are more trustees than staff?

Have a choccie, Abs.

ABI. No, thanks.

NICK. They're brown.

ABI. I could actually report you.

NICK *offers the calendar to* RYAN. ABI *keeps peering in the window.*

NICK. Have Christmas Day, Slave Labour. You've put a shift in today.

I used to love this time when I was a kid. Bedtime on Christmas Eve. It was amazing. I used to get so excited I'd run round the living room until I went dizzy and passed out.

My mum used to say it was at this time that Father
Christmas was deciding who had been good and who had
been bad. I used to confess to everything – stealing marbles
from Nigel Burwood, smashing the neighbour's greenhouse
with my football.

All so I could get an Ewok Village.

Gullible, wasn't I?

And I never got it but… suppose the anticipation's better
than /

ABI. Sssh! She's put the phone down. She's coming.

ABI *and* NICK *dart to their desks and pretend to be
working. Enter* PAT, *holding a folder. She puts the folder on
her desk.*

NICK. How was Chairman Cow?

PAT. Her name is Shelagh, Nick.

Well… there were a couple of hurdles. The board were
concerned about Green Crescent's experience but I explained
their forms were in order and they were endorsed by Oxfam.

But all in all, Shelagh's very pleased. All of the board are,
apparently.

They've approved the money transfer so we can set up the
payment, Abi.

ABI *opens up the correct file on her computer.*

ABI. Good to go here. Just type your password in there.

PAT *leans over and types in her password.*

PAT. There. And you'll approve it?

ABI (*talks as she types*). I'll log you out and log me in. (*Types
her password.*)

PAT *begins putting her coat on.*

PAT. All right, I'm going. John Lewis is still open isn't it?

RYAN. It's open until 9 p.m. for the duration of the Christmas period.

PAT. Then I've still got time to get something for Roger. He's back from Dubai and wants a tree to offset his air miles. John Lewis probably don't even do trees.

ABI. There. Money's gone.

NICK. Wicked!

(*Pulls up his email.*) Then we can get the press release… (*Presses send.*) Sent.

Ryan, website going live?

RYAN *presses a button on his keyboard.*

RYAN. Done.

NICK. We are launched. We have literally saved Pakistan.

PAT. Good. Well done again. I didn't think we'd do it but… we did.

NICK. Can we have an ironic high-five?

NICK *lays his palm out.*

RYAN. Do we have to?

NICK. Now I've laid it out there for ya. Don't leave me hanging.

RYAN *reluctantly slaps* NICK*'s palm.*

Abs?

ABI *reluctantly slaps* NICK*'s palm.* NICK *moves round to* PAT *who just stares at him. He lowers his hand back to his side.*

PAT *moves to exit.*

PAT. If Rory calls can you not tell him? I'd like to break the good news myself.

You'll be able to survive without me?

NICK. Dandy, Patricia. It's party time here now.

PAT *puts her gloves on.*

PAT. I hope not. We don't need any repeats of last night, do we? It smelt like an allotment in here this morning. It's the last time we organise fun.

Oxford Street is going to be an absolute nightmare.

NICK. Happy Christmas, Pat.

ABI. See you on the twenty-seventh.

RYAN. Bye.

PAT *ignores* RYAN *and exits.* NICK *goes to the door and makes sure* PAT *has left.*

NICK. Elvis has left the building.

NICK *rubs his hands and chuckles to himself. He goes to the filing cabinet and takes out three plastic cups. He gives one to each of them.*

ABI. What's this?

NICK *holds his finger up to say 'one moment'. He then goes to a different drawer and pulls out a Ribena bottle full of green liquid. He begins pouring each of them a cupful, disregarding their protests.*

NICK. The 2011 vintage. Brewed in Braintree and marinated in plastic. Granted it does have a legume-y aftertaste but savour the thick body and you may even be able to identify the manure used on the courgettes.

ABI. I don't really –

NICK. A toast, Abs. To us. For launching a campaign in nine hours.

We've been proper brilliant.

Cheers!

NICK *and* ABI *drink. It's like lighter fluid.*

That's even worse than last night.

ABI. It's like rotten feet.

Another.

NICK. Yeah?

ABI. Let's celebrate properly.

> ABI *laughs.* NICK *grins, adds more to her cup.* ABI *raises her cup. So do* NICK *and* RYAN.

> Cheers!

NICK. Cheers!

> ABI *and* NICK *drink.* RYAN *doesn't.*

ABI. Urrgh! That is actually the taste of death.

> I need water.

> *Exit* ABI *to kitchen.*

NICK. You not thirsty, Ryan?

RYAN. Maybe later. I'm up to my eyes in paperwork.

NICK. Full of vitamins. Good for the – (*Indicates spunk.*) You'll drink worse at uni.

> RYAN *sips the drink. He pulls a face. He looks for somewhere to pour the drink. He pours it into the pot plant on* ABI*'s desk.*

> Don't waste it, mate!

RYAN. It might help… it grow.

NICK. I hope so, fella. That's Robert.

RYAN. It's got a name?

NICK. Oh yeah. Robert. Plant. Her pride and joy that. If you kill it with moonshine… (*Indicates throat cutting.*)

> *The phone rings on* ABI*'s desk.* RYAN *picks it up.* NICK *puts the moonshine away.*

RYAN. Hi. Disasters Relief. Yeah. Yeah. She's not here at the moment. Can I take a message?

> Wait a minute.

> RYAN *shields the receiver.*

> Nick? Where's Abi? He says he wants to talk to her urgently.

NICK. Who is it?

RYAN. Erm, Sebastian Something.

NICK. Camp Bastian?

> Oh fuck. How's he sound? Like he wants to ram an eco-toilet up our arses?

> RYAN *shrugs,* NICK *points* RYAN *towards kitchen.* RYAN *exits.* NICK *flicks Vs at the phone. And then thrusts his groin at the receiver before picking up.*

> All right, Bastian, it's Nick Webb. (*Reply.*) How's Pakistan? (*Reply.*) Yeah?

> *Enter* ABI.

> She's back now, mate. Looking a bit peaky. Watch out for those aftershocks.

> ABI *mouths 'Who is it?' to* NICK. NICK *makes a 'wanker' sign.* NICK *passes the receiver to* ABI.

> (*Mutters.*) Hate for a mountain to fall on your massive head.

> NICK *watches and listens and* ABI *indicates that he should turn away. She turns her back.* NICK *returns to his desk and turns off his computer. Enter* RYAN *with a Fanta. As* ABI *is listening to Bastian,* NICK *puts his pens back in their holder, puts papers in his drawer, straightens his keyboard and…*

ABI. Bastian? Hi, it's Abi – (*Long reply.*) I know. I'm very sorry to hear that… what?

> *…then turns of his PC makes the 'shutdown' jingle.*

NICK. Happiest noise in the world that.

> NICK *crosses to the far side of the office and puts on his coat, scarf, gloves, etc., an eye on* ABI *but unable to hear her.*

ABI (*to Bastian*). What?… Who told you?

> (*Reply.*) …You're sure?… Right… right… Okay, we haven't, course we won't.

Thanks so much for letting me know. I really appreciate you taking the time to call.

Have a lovely Christmas. (*Reply*.) You too. Bye.

NICK *returns to his desk to pick his rucksack up.* ABI *puts the phone down.*

NICK. So, he forgiven us for flying solo?

ABI. What? Oh no, he's dead cool… he's got contacts coming out of his ears.

NICK. Sweet-talked him round?

ABI. Oh yeah. He's still in the fan club.

NICK. Right. I'm hitting the road. Get home. Stick the old stocking up.

I could wait if you

Want to –

Snifter for the road?

ABI. No, I don't think any more drink is a good idea.

NICK. At least I'll walk you to the Tube.

ABI. Better wait for Jaz to call back.

NICK. Right you'll lock up then?

ABI. Yeah.

NICK. Ryan, are you –?

RYAN. I'm still uploading to the website.

NICK. Okay.

I'll say goodnight then.

ABI. Yeah. Goodnight.

NICK. Happy Christmas.

RYAN. Happy Christmas.

ABI. Happy Christmas.

As NICK *exits…*

NICK. Well done, Abs. Seriously.

ABI. Thank you, Nick.

> *Exit* NICK. ABI *goes to the door to see if* NICK *has left.*
> RYAN *watches, nervous.*

> Fuck. Fuck. Fuck.

> ABI *rushes over to* PAT*'s computer.*

> Do you know Pat's password, Ryan?

RYAN. No, what's wrong?

ABI. She must have told it you.

RYAN. For her machine?

ABI. No, banking, our bank account.

RYAN. Erm…?

ABI. What would it be? Guess.

RYAN. Try 'password'? Or 123456.

ABI. Trying that. No. Anything else?

> RYAN *shakes his head.*

> What's the bank's number?

RYAN. Erm –

ABI. Don't worry I've got it.

> ABI *picks up the phone and calls the bank.*

RYAN. – ?

ABI. Don't just stand there. Try and log in. Anything you can think of. Her surname. Or 'Downton'.

> (*Into phone.*) Come on, come on!

> RYAN *sits at* PAT*'s desk and types in some passwords.*

> (*Into phone.*) Hello, hello?

> Stupid automated voices!

> (*To* RYAN.) Anything?

RYAN. I could call her?

ABI (*responding to phone*). Zero.

(*To* RYAN.) Do not call her.

ABI *presses zero on her machine*.

(*Into phone*.) How can you be closed?

Shit.

RYAN *shakes his head*.

RYAN. What's happened?

Abi?

ABI. I need to cancel the payment.

RYAN. Why?

ABI. It's Green Crescent. They kicked out Abdul Salim six months ago. He's not a director. He's a gunrunner. And he's got our money. We've given twenty-six grand to the Taliban.

ACT TWO

Scene One

9.02 a.m. 27th December.

The office has been cleaned and tidied since the last working day. Christmas decorations remain up.

ABI sits at her desk, phone receiver to her ear. RYAN stands next to the door to Rory's office, one eye on what's going on inside, one eye on ABI.

ABI. Still good?

RYAN. They're still talking. Pat's talking. Nick's nodding.

ABI *(into phone)*. Come on, come on!

(*To* RYAN.) They're supposed to open at nine.

I tried Boxing Day but /

(Into phone.) Hi. *(Reply.)* Hi George. My name's / Abi Ahmed.

It's a business account, yes. But listen, it's something very specific.

(Reply.) No, George, we're not interested in a premium account. I want to speak to you about a payment. *(Reply.)* Can you put your script down and listen? It's really urgent. *(Reply.)*

Yes, I've had a lovely Christmas thank you. Actually no I haven't. My fiancé threw me out. So I've been back in Yorkshire. *(Reply.)* You weren't to know. *(Reply.)* He stacked everything I have on the pavement outside his flat so. In boxes, in alphabetical order. Nice touch that, don't you think? *(Reply.)*

No, I don't want to change our joint account.

I want to stop a payment on a business account. Disasters Relief. 396702. (*Reply.*) 02378561. Can you do that?

Pause. RYAN *indicates that the meeting is nearly finished.*

(*Reply.*) Yes, twenty-six thousand. I want to cancel it.

(*Reply.*) Why not? There must be something you... it's gone to the wrong person.

(*Reply.*) I would have done if you'd been open. I know you're not HSBC but... the only reason we're with you is because you're ethical and if you can't cancel this then –

(*Reply.*) Okay. Okay. There's no way? You don't know what this means for us. (*Reply.*) Can I speak to your manager then? (*Short reply.*) No? (*Reply.*) No, I don't want police. Thank you.

ABI *hangs up.*

RYAN. They're finishing. What now?

ABI. If you've any ideas I'm all ears.

Santa didn't give you a time machine?

RYAN. Cushions.

My mum bought me cushions. And a spice rack.

ABI. I could smother myself with a cushion.

RYAN. When are you going to tell Pat?

ABI *shakes her head.*

ABI. I can't. If I tell Pat, she tells the board. The board tell the Charity Commission. We get shut down. Everyone loses their jobs.

RYAN. But –

ABI. And who do you think will get blamed? Me. The muslim girl who sent money to terrorists.

We can sort this out.

RYAN. We?

ABI. Yeah, 'we'.

We're a team, Ryan.

You said you wanted to help?

RYAN. I know but

I haven't been able to think about anything else. Christmas Day was a nightmare. My gran was asking me what I'd been doing here. And I had to lie. To my gran.

ABI. It'll be fine. But she – (*Points towards* PAT*'s desk.*) can't know anything's wrong. I need you to buy us time. Can you do that?

RYAN. Erm –

Enter NICK *from Rory's office.*

ABI. Sssh.

RYAN returns to his desk.

NICK. Hey, Abs, you made it in then.

ABI. My sister drove us down from Bradford.

NICK. Early one then.

ABI. 5.30.

NICK enters the stationery cupboard.

NICK. Ow! How was it then, your Christmas?

ABI. Amazing, you?

NICK (*from inside the cupboard*). You know, three nights of wink murder, Dad farting into the couch. And my nan licking turkey off the inside of her gum plate.

Apart from that.

ABI (*to* RYAN). Jump on the website yeah and delete anything that mentions Abdul Salim or Green Crescent. And then delete posts on Facebook and any tweets.

NICK enters, holding some A4 printed photographs. He begins pinning the prints – of tents and villagers in the affected villages in Pakistan – up on the wall or spreading them across his desk.

NICK. Standard fare really.

ABI. Nightmare.

(*To* RYAN.) Okay?

RYAN *nods. Enter* PAT.

PAT. Morning, Abi – (*Looks at the clock.*) Have you started the progress report?

ABI. Pardon?

PAT. We'll need a progress report for the board. Shelagh's incredibly excited and wants to see what our money's been spent on.

ABI. Erm, okay. We'll get started.

PAT. She needs it by three. With everything. Quotes, statistics –

Everything you can get from Mr Salim.

ABI (*to* RYAN). You can help me with that, Ryan?

RYAN. Me?

ABI. Yeah.

RYAN. What about the… [deleting]

PAT. It's a problem?

RYAN. No?

PAT. Thank you. A can-do attitude at last.

ABI *sits at her desk.* RYAN *at his desk.* PAT *takes over the pinning.* NICK *picks up a charity gift pack.*

NICK. Nice chrizzie present, Pat.

Very handsome fella, I've gotta say.

PAT. It's a 'she'.

NICK. She's got a lovely beard.

PAT. And her name's Edith.

NICK. Edith? Nice name.

PAT. Not for a goat.

NICK. Yeah but –

PAT. Tethered to a dead tree in the Sudanese desert. She looks half-starved.

Honestly, it's the last time we do an ethical Christmas. Roger said it was a choice between that or a portable toilet. He thought Edith was more me.

NICK. She does have your eyes.

PAT. No she does not, Nick.

NICK. And a lovely coat.

PAT. To think I bought him a new bicycle. And Pippa, we got an iPad. But how that's going to reduce her carbon footprint…

NICK. Bet old Roge didn't just get you a goat though?

PAT. There was that too.

PAT *points to her shawl, draped over the back of her chair.*
NICK *puts the pack down and picks up the shawl.*

NICK. This is more like it! Very swish, Pat. Very nice. This must have eaten into his golfing fund.

PAT. It's Hermès, he said. He brought it back from Dubai.

NICK. Very nice.

PAT. I'm not sure. Look at the label.

NICK *looks at the label.*

NICK. Ooh. Made in the People's Republic of China.

PAT. The thought of it being made in a sweatshop really… it doesn't, well –

It's not ideal is it.

NICK. What is though? Everything I'm wearing's probably been made by blind orphans with no teeth. All this furniture.

PAT *takes the shawl from* NICK.

PAT. Nick, don't! It's not something I want to think about. I feel guilty enough using all this paper.

NICK. Just joshing. It's lovely that.

PAT. You think?

PAT *admires the shawl.*

NICK. Yeah. What about you, Ryan? Like it?

RYAN. Er, what? Yeah.

NICK. There you go. Voice of the fashion police.

(*To* PAT.) Suits you.

PAT *smiles.*

PAT. I'll keep it, I think.

RYAN (*joke*). And take back the goat.

PAT. You can't take back a goat. It's in Africa.

PAT *turns back to the pictures.*

No, it's no good, I can't see them anywhere.

Abi?

PAT *beckons* ABI *over and then looks carefully at the photos on the wall.*

I can't see any of our tents in these photos. We've looked through the stills from AP and Nick's been through the press. We should be in some, a couple at least.

ABI. Where were they taken?

NICK. Everywhere. Challa Bandi. Patan. There's twenty thousand people living under tents.

PAT. And not one of them ours.

ABI. There must be.

PAT. You can look. But you won't see any.

NICK. I thought you told Green Crescent to use our logo?

ABI. I did.

PAT. Can you speak to your man and tell him branding is important.

NICK. Visibility, Abs.

ABI. Sure. They must have not / got it.

PAT. It's got to be on every tent. And in white. So it can be seen.

ABI. I'll keep chasing Mr Salim.

PAT. Yes, now, Abi. And your progress report by this afternoon remember.

ABI. Sure. No problem. No problem at all.

PAT. All right, knock when it's ready.

PAT *exits.* ABI *returns to her desk.* NICK *follows and sits at his desk.*

NICK. Suppose you haven't heard the news? My little press release has got major bites. Rory's on his way to Manchester for a 5-live phone-in.

ABI. Congratulations. It's thrilling to see you in such a good mood.

NICK. Am I?

ABI. You were flirting with Pat.

NICK. That was not flirting.

ABI. It really was. I had a bit of sick come up.

NICK. I was just spreading a bit of the Nick Webb charm.

ABI. Nick, Lynx Africa isn't charm.

NICK. Ha, you say that. But she loved it, you see her?

ABI. She went all gooey and girly. It was a bit – (*Shivers.*)

NICK. It's the effect I have. I'm irresistible to her.

ABI. Yeah, like an HRT patch.

NICK. You seen her like that before?

ABI. Once. When she met Nigel Havers in Pret. She went red and made a joke about his banana.

NICK *opens up the Disasters Relief web page and pays it fleeting attention.*

NICK. She's chuffed. Despite getting a goat. It's the campaign. Grade-A success and she knows it.

ABI. Thanks to your publicity. I guess you're back to being golden-bollocks.

NICK. Abs, I'm just the messenger. You are golden-bollocks.

ABI. I really am not.

NICK. Mate, we were up and out before a single one of the big boys. I heard Jeremy Allen at Merlin went mental, mouthing off about us 'getting above ourselves'.

Now, you just make sure your report's full of nice juicy pics of your Green Crescent lads saving poor freezing locals /

ABI. With the tents.

NICK. In our nice branded tents. The board will love it, the funders will love it.

ABI *smiles painfully.*

You're Head Girl.

Scene Two

11.39 a.m. 27th December.

RYAN *sits at his desk working on the progress report.* ABI *sits at her desk reading through the results of a Google search about Abdul Salim, while calling Abdul Salim on her mobile. No answer. She hangs up.*

RYAN. Still nothing?

ABI. No. Just a dead tone. And my emails are bouncing back. He's disappeared.

RYAN. Maybe he might still give them the money?

ABI. We can dream. But, no, he'll have bolted into the tribal regions. That whole border area is completely lawless. Right now, our money's being spent on guns, drugs, anything.

RYAN. We don't know that though.

ABI. No we do. (*Pointing to her screen.*) He's on the Home Office proscribed list. Which I would have seen, if I'd checked. But I didn't check. Why did I rush it? I'm such an idiot.

RYAN. You're not. You're like pretty awesome.

ABI. No, I'm not. In one day I sent money to terrorists and got dumped by my fiancé. And I have no idea how to make any of it better.

Pause.

RYAN. But look what I've done.

RYAN *points to his PC screen which shows the Disasters Relief website.*

I've replaced every reference to Green Crescent with the word 'partners'. And deleted all the photos and links and references to donations and tents.

ABI. And?

RYAN. Pat and Nick haven't noticed anything so far.

ABI. At all?

RYAN *shakes his head.*

Okay okay so how about, if we think this through, then we could… no… I suppose no one's noticed so far… so maybe we could see how it goes for a while like this and…

RYAN. Do nothing?

ABI. Maybe?

If we can see this out then, and our campaign is nearly over, we can… see, a normal campaign, yeah, is a month. Assessment, shipment, delivery, results. We're already at results so –

RYAN. So?

ABI. So we're nearly done. We wait it out. In a week's time there'll be another disaster. A flood in Africa, a quake in Iran. We'll move on and this'll be forgotten. And we can deliver ten thousand tents. Next time.

And that'll balance this out.

Like a kind of… see-saw.

Of good and bad. And the good will – (*Mimes the good outweighing bad.*)

Yeah?

RYAN. But –

ABI. It makes me a terrible human being.

RYAN. Yes, I mean no.

I mean, the results for the progress report. How do we – ?

ABI. Get them? Maybe we – ?

RYAN. We don't write them in?

ABI. That's it. This is the same disaster in the same place as last time. And we've done the same response so –

ABI *picks up the 2005 report from her desk.*

RYAN. We'll write the same report?

ABI. This is the 2005 report. It's on the shared drive. I'll do the intro and evaluation. You amend the stats and change the pictures.

RYAN. But we haven't got any other pictures.

ABI. Go on to Google. Photoshop the logos onto tents. And make up quotes from victims. Be creative.

RYAN. I don't do creative.

ABI. Then now's your chance to learn.

The website's public: keep it saying nothing.

This – (*The report*.) is just internal. It's only got to get past Pat, Rory and the board.

RYAN *stares back like a rabbit in the headlights. Enter* NICK, *on his mobile. He sits in his chair.*

NICK (*into phone, posh voice*). Simon, I hear you, I do. And I know it's not front-page stuff but this is a cracking piece for the *Guardian*. We are only five people and we've got twenty-six grand's worth of tents out there before any other charity. (*Reply*.) Unicef? Not done a thing. (*Reply*.) We're first. (*Reply*.)

Our Humanitarian Manager Pat Williams. (*Reply*.) Yeah? A profile piece the Society pages?

Yeah, you can find all the details on our web page. It's disasters relief dot /

NICK *sees that the web page has changed.*

One second, Simon.

NICK *puts his hand over the phone.*

Ryan mate, all your stuff's gone walkabout on our website.

RYAN. Has it?

NICK. Yeah, look.

RYAN looks at NICK's *screen. Then looks to* ABI.

RYAN. Oh yeah.

NICK. Where the hell is it? We been hacked or something? This is the *Guardian*, mate. He's – (*Simon.*) gonna need this.

NICK stands and gets RYAN *to sit in his seat.*

Get onto there and stick it all back up yeah.

And double-check our Facebook and Twitter feeds.

Quick as you can, mate.

(*Into phone.*) Sorry, Simon. Couple of spotty gremlins in our IT system.

Yeah, let me get Pat's diary and get a time for you.

Exit NICK *into Rory's office.* RYAN *turns to* ABI, *scared.*

RYAN. What do I do?

ABI. Do not do any retweeting or Facebook.

RYAN. But he said to.

ABI. I know but –

RYAN. He'll see. And then Pat'll see and then the journalist –

ABI. Ryan, just update the website but don't mention Green Crescent.

RYAN. How?

ABI. Use your initiative, Ryan. And keep deleting.

RYAN. I can't keep deleting Green Crescent if I'm adding them too.

We're gonna get found out.

ABI. We're not.

RYAN. I knew this would happen. Last night I couldn't sleep. Or the night before. I just sat up watching QVC. I almost bought a tumble dryer.

ABI. Look, it's /

RYAN. How will I look my gran in the eye?

She fought in the war. I've armed the Taliban.

We're supposed to be good.

ABI. We are. But see, charity isn't black and white. We're not always doing the right thing.

RYAN (*incredulous*). Like all the time?

ABI. Sometimes it's murky. In Darfur, yeah, we housed refugees escaping the Janjaweed. And we knew some of the 'refugees' sleeping in our tents were probably the Janjaweed in disguise. So we had to make a call. Do we save murderers for the sake of saving the innocent.

Look at Pakistan. We rush over there, patch up the country, while the Government – which is one of the most corrupt on earth – stands idly by. They barely do anything to stop these floods and quakes and they kill thousands every single time. So by helping, we help prop up their regime.

RYAN. So maybe it's a good thing to do nothing?

ABI. Exactly.

No. I don't know.

Everything feels really confused.

Before Christmas I thought I knew where I was: where my life was going, what I believed. But now –

RYAN. Maybe we should just tell Pat.

ABI (*shakes her head*). I can't. She's worked here twenty years. She loves this company.

RYAN. Mrs Boxall says telling the truth is always best.

ABI. Ryan, I don't know who this Mrs Boxall is but she's not bloody Oprah. You don't have to do everything she says.

RYAN. But if I do what you say or Nick says, it all goes wrong. You should do what's right. You know what's right in here – (*Indicates heart.*)

ABI. I tried that at the party. And it all went wrong.

You can't trust this – (*Heart.*) We have to think it through logically.

You don't get it, Ryan. Sometimes it's okay to compromise and to settle for… what's not quite right. You might not be happy but you'll be secure and that's more important cos you might be happy in the future and it's okay to believe that isn't it?

Enter NICK.

NICK. That's the *Grauniad* in the bag.

Beat.

Oh, bit awks. Have I walked into something?

Lovers' tiff?

RYAN. No!

ABI. No. We were talking about the report.

RYAN. I was saying it didn't matter if it was wrong.

We should settle for second best.

NICK. Really?

RYAN. Yes. Even if you know in your heart it'll crush you.

NICK. Have a word, Abs. You can't settle for second best.

Reach for the stars, mate. Seven famous philosophers said that.

RYAN *looks pointedly at* ABI.

Get this, Pat's gonna be in the *Guardian*. Rory's all over the BBC. We're cleaning up. I'm not saying the Charity Awards are in the bag or nothing but… every judge is gonna be reading about us tomorrow.

ABI *smiles. Then looks at* RYAN. *Who looks at* NICK.

Scene Three

2.39 p.m. 27th December.

PAT *sits at her desk applying lipstick.* RYAN *arranges the report on the floor, placing pages one at a time in piles. He is beginning to panic at times, stops and stares into the distance.*

NICK *is on the phone to Rory. He stands in front of the TV with the remote and skips from coverage of the earthquake – with headlines now reading 'ESTIMATED 6,500 DEAD' and 'AFTERSHOCKS OF 5.6 RICHTER SCALE. CHOLERA OUTBREAK'.*

NICK. Rory Rory, hey, how's Salford, sir? (*Short reply.*) Till when? Right, okay. (*Short reply.*) Is she? Ha, that's good. Very good. (*Short reply.*) That's just inappropriate. Even in the seventies. Don't say that to her or anyone with a microphone.

(*Longer reply about* PAT.) Yeah yeah she knows. She's delighted. Cheers bye.

PAT. I really don't know about this.

NICK. You'll be incredible, Pat. With your charm.

PAT. But Rory always does the interviews. I've never done one before. I don't know what to say.

NICK. Yeah yeah but he's up in Manc Land all day.

PAT. Okay, tell me who this man is then.

NICK. Simon Cotterall. He's lovely and fluffy and he's been on the *Guardian* for years, the sort of man you'd want your disabled daughter to meet.

PAT. Pippa's not disabled.

NICK. He'll be lovely to you. And it's just a quarter page in the Society section.

PAT. What will he ask?

NICK. About the campaign. What we've done. How we're so much better than Bastian and his seven dwarves.

He's one of us, Pat. The *Guardian* are our people.

The door buzzer beeps.

That'll be him now.

PAT *quickly applies more make-up*. RYAN *listens in*.

Just remember. It's David and Goliath. We're a quick, nimble, modern charity different from the rusty old giants. It's really important he gets that. Because this is all for the funders.

PAT (*mutters*). Funders.

NICK. We're the future. We're the ones they should be pouring money into. You've got that?

PAT. Yes, yes.

Bell rings again.

I better go.

NICK. You've got the meeting room downstairs till five.

If he needs more information, he can jump on our website, yeah, Ryan?

NICK *hands* PAT *a piece of paper with bullet points about the campaign*. RYAN *doesn't respond. Bell rings again.* PAT *picks up her pashmina.*

PAT. Should I wear this?

NICK. Looks classy, Pat.

PAT. He won't know, will he?

NICK. You can't even see the bloody handprints. Go go.

She puts it on and exits.

That is all right, mate? The website's back to normal?

Mate?

Ryan?

NICK *takes a moment to watch* RYAN. RYAN *takes another piece of paper and puts it down near the other one.*

You er all right, Slave Labour?

RYAN. Yes. Thank you.

NICK. Sure?

RYAN *picks up another piece of paper from his desk and puts it in a different place in the room.* NICK *watches all this.*

NICK *passes* RYAN *a box of Sainsbury's mini-brownies.*

Have a team treat.

RYAN. No thank you.

NICK. They're brownies, mate.

RYAN. I know but five years of brownies and I'll end up like [you]

Unhealthy.

NICK. Don't worry about that. You've got fifty more years of this, shuffling paper. All for a gradually decreasing wage and piss-poor pension.

NICK *picks up the report.*

This Abi's progress report, is it?

RYAN. A summary of the campaign so far. Money spent, resources purchased and distributed. And feedback from earthquake victims.

NICK *flicks through it.*

NICK. These pictures from Kashmir?

RYAN. Yes.

What?

NICK (*unsure*). Nothing. I couldn't find any tents with our logo on.

And people said that?

NICK *leafs through the report to near the end.*

Bit light, don't you think? Thought there'd be more stats and stuff. If I give this to the *Guardian* they'll use it for bog roll.

RYAN. The *Guardian*? I thought this was just for Pat and the board?

NICK. No. We want maximum publicity. I'm gonna send this to every hack I know.

RYAN *looks scared.*

What's up?

RYAN. Nothing.

NICK. Come on, tell Uncle Nick.

RYAN. It's nothing, I said.

NICK. You can tell us, we're mates.

RYAN. Are we?

NICK. Yeah yeah. You've done brilliant on all the web stuff.

You're part of the comms team as far as I'm [concerned], you know.

So what is it? Has Abi been taking the piss out of your hair again?

RYAN. Does she?

NICK. No! It's a joke.

Your hair is lovely.

RYAN. It's really nothing.

NICK. You deleted the shared drive?

RYAN. No.

NICK. Lost your passcard?

RYAN. What?

NICK. Virginity?

RYAN. What? No!

NICK. So?!

RYAN. It's –

Like –

Why do you do this job?

NICK. Communications?

RYAN. Charity.

NICK. You thinking of it? We inspired you?

RYAN. I was thinking very seriously about it. But I've

I'm not sure any more.

NICK. My case, mate, I used to do comms for Vodafone, massive corporation, making millions, who pay fuck-all tax yeah. I was making tidy money but I had this moment where I thought 'What the hell am I doing?', dedicating my life to helping those people line their pockets.

I thought I wanna look myself in the mirror when I'm ninety-five and go 'Yeah, you weren't just a drain on this planet. You didn't spend all your life going up the property ladder and buying iPhones and Audis. You sheltered thousands after the cyclone in India and you put an arm round kids whose mums had died in Syria.' I dunno, might sound a bit Bono that, but I don't care.

It's what it's all about.

RYAN. Being good?

NICK. It's important isn't it?

RYAN. What if you don't do good? Like, if you found out what you were doing was bad. What would you do?

NICK. Depends how bad.

RYAN. Like really bad.

What if like, you were the one that was –

NICK. If I did something?

RYAN. Yeah. Or helped someone.

NICK. Do something wrong?

RYAN. Yeah.

NICK. Someone you know?

> RYAN *nods*.
>
> Like a mate from school or – ?
>
> RYAN *shakes his head*.
>
> Or brother?
>
> Someone who you… work with?

RYAN. Yeah.

NICK. Here?

RYAN. –

NICK. Mate?

RYAN. It's nothing. I meant like hypothetically. What would you do?

NICK. Erm, the right thing I hope.

RYAN. But if you didn't know what the right thing was.

NICK. I'd ask someone more experienced. Which in your case would be me.

RYAN. –

NICK. And they'd ask what the problem was.

> And I'd say… what it was.

RYAN. But if you couldn't.

NICK. Then I'd at least give them a sense of how serious it was.

> RYAN *rubs his hair, hard*.

RYAN. God. Yeah.

> NICK *indicates small with his finger and thumb*.

NICK. This serious?

RYAN. God, no. Really I shouldn't. Forget I said anything.

NICK. Ryan?

> NICK *indicates small with his finger and thumb.* RYAN *shakes his head.* NICK *makes the space bigger.* RYAN *shakes his head. They repeat once more.* NICK *indicates his surprise.*

> *Enter* ABI *with a plastic cup of water. She tends her plant.*

ABI (*breezily*). Hi.

> RYAN *freezes.*

> All right?

RYAN. Yeah.

> ABI *looks at* NICK *and smiles.*

ABI. You all right?

NICK. Oh yeah. Like Jimmy Savile in Mothercare. Just reading through the progress report. Bit thin isn't it?

ABI. It's a progress report, Nick. We'll add more info when we've made more progress, obviously.

> ABI *turns to her computer, her back to* NICK *and* RYAN. NICK *starts from where he left off with* RYAN.

NICK. That's not normal is it?

> NICK *increases the size of the space.* RYAN *shakes his head, looking at* ABI.

ABI. Pat wants it quickly so it's going to be short. And with lots of charts and pictures, it'll help Shelagh with the long words.

> NICK *increases the size of the space. He's now got his arms opened.* RYAN *shakes his head, looking at* ABI.

NICK. And you'll be all right to get it finished will you?

ABI. Oh yeah. Ryan's helping me with it.

> NICK *now has his arms spread as wide as he can.*

NICK. Is that right, Ryan?

RYAN. Yeah.

NICK (*mouths to* RYAN). Fuck.

> NICK *sees how panicked* RYAN *looks. He releases his arms.*

> I know what you mean.

> RYAN *puts his finger to his lips.* NICK *shakes his head.*

> Too late, mate.

ABI. We're fine. I'm finishing off the evaluation now.

NICK. I better do something.

> RYAN *shakes his head.*

ABI. You can help Ryan collate it. You'll like work. It gives you an enormous sense of well-being.

> The difference between try and triumph is a little umph.

NICK. Abi?

ABI. Get this report done and the project's near finished.

> ABI *turns round and sees* RYAN *and* NICK. *She looks at* RYAN. RYAN *looks back, terrified.*

> What have you?

> Have you – ?

> ABI *looks to* NICK.

> Did he –?

> NICK *nods.*

> It's not what you think.

Scene Four

2.59 p.m. 27th December.

NICK *is hiding under his desk, with his knees pulled up to his chin.* ABI *stands next to his desk, attempting to coax him out.*

RYAN *watches*.

ABI. Nick! You've got to come out and /

NICK. No shitting chance, Abs; I'm staying right here. Where my nuts are safe.

ABI. Pat's not going to hurt you.

NICK. This is like… Jesus, Abs, this is so… this is like finding you're behind Hitler in the Human Centipede.

ABI. It massively isn't.

NICK. Isn't it!? How!?

ABI. Come out and we'll tell you.

NICK. Not even for diplomatic immunity.

ABI. You're not bloody Julian Assange.

It's all okay. I'm putting everything right.

NICK. The money's gone, Salim's not calling back! The *Titanic*'s sunk and you're Winslet floating on a door.

ABI. Listen, the campaign continues as planned. 'Green Crescent' message us to say how successful their mission was. You say we're delighted on our website and we thank our donors.

In a month's time, there's another disaster, another campaign, and this incident is ancient history.

NICK *emerges*.

NICK. Until Green Crescent do, I dunno, a search of the net? And find us. Then call us asking how they gave out tents when we gave them no money.

ABI. It might work out.

NICK. Bastian might be wrong? How do we know Salim is crooked?

ABI. The Home Office, he said.

NICK. Fuck!

ABI. Remember the Dodgy Dossier.

NICK fetches and opens a packet of Mini Cheddars.

NICK. That was the invasion of Iraq. We're supplying sleeping bags. The Home Office don't need to lie about this.

If Salim's a gunrunner, Abs, we've given him twenty-six grand.

If all of that money is spent on guns then we're helping them kill people. Probably innocent people. And if they're crossing into Afghanistan then it's probably innocent British soldiers.

ABI. I know, I know!

NICK. 'Lefty do-gooders arm the Taliban'. We're the *Daily Mail*'s wet dream.

Simon Cotterall is gonna have our nuts.

ABI. I know all of that.

NICK. We're fucked. We're gonna spend the rest of our lives sorting piss-stained pants in Oxfam shops.

Beat.

I'm finding Pat.

ABI. No!

NICK. It's your contact, your decision, your fuck-up.

I go along with this and it goes tits up, I'm fucked too.

I come clean, change the partner, I'm Head Girl.

ABI. You wouldn't though.

NICK. Why not?

ABI. Cos... cos we're... [friends]

NICK. We're what, Abs?

I don't know any more.

ABI. I...

NICK. – ?

ABI. –

NICK. You're supposed to be the quality one.

I'm the one who fucks stuff up, who's always late and says the wrong thing to the wrong people.

We're supposed to be mates. At the very least. And mates tell each other stuff.

Do I not mean nothing to you? No?

Beat.

Then we're going on shutdown.

ABI. What?!

NICK. This is September eleventh. We're taking down the planes and shutting the airports. Ryan, put all phones on DND and lock the doors.

ABI. What are you – ?

NICK. Sorry, Abs, you don't get a say in this. I'm applying sanctions.

RYAN *begins putting the phones on 'Do Not Disturb'. He locks the doors.*

ABI. What?

NICK. Yep. You're dangerous, Abi. You're like a rogue state.

ABI. That's stupid.

NICK. Ryan, you're the UN. Get your blue hat on. Get under that desk and unplug her machine.

ABI. Nick!

NICK. Go on, mate, chop-chop.

> RYAN *looks between* ABI *and* NICK.

ABI. Don't.

NICK. Do it.

ABI. This is so stupid.

NICK. No no, this is necessary.

> NICK *indicates that* RYAN *should do it.* RYAN *ducks under* ABI*'s desk.*

> Unplug it at the socket. And the phone while you're at it.

ABI. Nick, I can solve this.

NICK. By coming clean to Pat?

ABI. No.

NICK. Getting the money back?

> Getting other money?

ABI. No.

NICK. Until then, Abs, you ent doing any more damage.

> You all done, Ryan?

> RYAN *backs out.*

RYAN. Sorry.

NICK. Don't apologise to her.

ABI. It's all right. It's not you being a twat.

NICK. It is one hundred per cent not me.

> I'm protecting this company from being obliterated. This isn't just a shitstorm. This is a turd the size of fucking Swindon falling on us like a swimming pool of runny shit.

> Ryan mate, I want you to watch her like a hawk. If she tries to plug her machine in, stop her. If she tries to leave follow her, if she makes calls on this [mobile], listen in.

If she gets abusive make a note. Everything she says.

Who knows what we might need as evidence. As war crimes.

ABI. My God, you actually think you're David Cameron.

NICK. Wait, do not call me a Tory.

ABI. You've got the same sanctimony. That Western-white-man thing.

NICK. I'm not the whole of the fucking Western world.

ABI. You're acting like it. The interfering, the taking over, the sanctions, the making us feel like pariahs.

NICK. Who's 'us'?

ABI. Us in the East.

NICK. You're the whole of Asia?

ABI. It is my heritage.

Like yours in Tory Berkshire.

NICK. I suppose you are like Pakistan. In that you've funded terrorists. And we can't trust you.

ABI. And we can't trust you. If you wanna know why our work out East is a nightmare, this is why. Cos we know this is what you're like.

NICK. Maybe we should call it a day then, East and West. Lead separate lives?

ABI. Maybe.

Look, I made a mistake. I haven't denied the Holocaust. Or reanimated Bin Laden.

Beat.

NICK. You can save that for your next trick.

(*Thinking aloud.*) What am I gonna do?

ABI. Don't tell Pat.

NICK. Do not worry, that is your job. If you still have one.

ABI. You can't tell her.

NICK. She gets told last. By you, and only when I'm at home and out of range.

> We need to get Cotterall out of here. How are we gonna do that?

RYAN. Hostages?

NICK. What?

RYAN. I... I thought we could take him hostage but that's [stupid]... maybe set off the fire alarm?

ABI. Let them publish.

NICK. Abs, if they publish some expert out there, some Foreign Office wonk who reads the *Graun* every morning, will read it and go 'Oh Green Crescent, is that who Abdul Salim worked for... oh blow me, it is. I think I better tell someone.'

ABI. They might not.

NICK. They really really really will.

> And if not them, then Bastian. You've got to call Bastian now. Before he finds out from someone else. And get him to keep schtum.
>
> NICK *takes a deep breath and picks up the report.*
>
> Okay, okay, this report wouldn't convince his (RYAN*'s.*) blind granny. So they're getting shredded.
>
> (*To* ABI.) You do a new report about Green Crescent and tents.
>
> (*To* RYAN.) You update the website with no mention of Green Crescent. But do mention tents.
>
> Then I'll go downstairs, get rid of Simon and his notes about Abdul Salim, Green Crescent and tents.
>
> Fuck.

Scene Five

3.30 p.m. 27th December.

ABI *sits at her desk.* NICK *watches as* RYAN *runs the reports through the shredder.*

NICK. Why is this so slow? It's like one page a minute.

We've got to get another one. Or hamsters. Ryan, ring a pet shop and get them to deliver a hundred gerbils. We'll feed them speed and they can eat the evidence.

RYAN. Is there a pet shop near here?

NICK. No, it was a joke. Like everything in this shitting office.

What's the time?

RYAN. Half past three.

NICK. I need to go and find Cotterall and Pat. What am I gonna say?

Abi, what about Bastian?

ABI *writes 'no answer' on a Post-it and hands it to* RYAN.

RYAN. She says 'no answer'.

NICK. Can she try again then?

ABI *writes '3 times' on a Post-it and hands it to* RYAN. *She picks up the phone and dials.*

RYAN. She says she's tried three times.

ABI *indicates that she's calling.*

And she's trying again.

ABI *(into phone).* Hi, Bastian, it's Abi Ahmed from Disasters Relief. How are you again? Like I've said, it's about Abdul Salim so… I really really need your help. Call me back now please. Bye.

RYAN *picks up his pad*.

RYAN. Shall I write 'no answer'?

ABI. If you have to.

RYAN (*writes*). I'll write it under the other 'no answer'.

Nick, Abi had no answer from Bastian Ridley.

ABI. Twice.

RYAN. Twice.

NICK. Weird cos I thought he really fancied you.

ABI. Guess not. Another one who doesn't. I might start a list.

NICK *picks up the pieces of shredded paper and stuffs them into a black bin liner*.

ABI *runs out of Post-it notes*. ABI *goes to speak to* NICK. *He notices so gives her a pad of Post-it notes from* PAT*'s desk.* ABI *takes them and lobs them to the other side of the room*.

NICK. Erm?

ABI. I'm not spending the rest of today talking via sticky paper.

NICK *shrugs*.

And how am I going to write a new report if my computer's unplugged?

NICK. All right.

NICK *plugs her computer into the mains*.

ABI. You're handling this like a child. You honestly think this is the best way?

NICK. Ha.

ABI. Excuse me?

NICK. You, saying 'honestly'. Sort of sounds hollow, from you.

ABI. Me? I'm honest.

NICK. Not honest enough to tell me.

ABI. Why would I tell you?

NICK. Cos we've worked together for four years. We are friends. And, madly, I thought 'more than friends'.

ABI. 'More than friends'? But you're not interested.

NICK. When did I ever say that?

ABI. What you said to Ryan, on Christmas Eve.

NICK. Eh?

ABI. Ryan? Tell him what he said to you.

RYAN. Erm. I don't know if I should –

ABI. S'all right, tell him.

RYAN. On Christmas Eve, before I said, when I didn't say, coloured. I said 'You're not properly into her then' and you said –

NICK. Yeah?

RYAN. 'I'm not in love with Abi.'

NICK. No, but... I was... that was only cos he... and cos you had said 'last night never happened'.

ABI. Because I was angry.

NICK. Because we slept –

RYAN *creeps out to the kitchen.*

ABI. No, because of your text message.

NICK. Which I only sent –

ABI. Because of Jaz.

NICK. Because of what you said.

At the party. We were in there – (*Rory's office.*) And I kissed your head. And you held my hands. And you said, Abs, you said.

In another world... you could... we would –

And I said – [the same].

ABI. I remember.

NICK. I meant it. I thought you did too?

ABI. I did. About him, that bloke, that Nick from Christmas Eve. He made me feel amazing cos he cared. He listened to me. Made me feel me.

NICK. Yeah, I did, I mean I do.

ABI. But actually now, this Nick, he's a bit of a knob who spazzes out and cuts off my phone and makes me talk to him in Post-it notes.

NICK. Abs, I do –

ABI. What?

NICK. No, I mean, I'm that me, the me before. Not the spazzy one, the good bloke one, cos see, you are special… you're the most beautiful special funny fuckin' smart person who is so fucking, who's so just given twenty-six grand to the Taliban and is gonna make me lose my job and ruin my whole life.

ABI. And you, you're the one who's funny and sweet and generous and who's just broken up my home and made me feel like I don't know who I am so my life is in pieces.

NICK. You are… so –

ABI. And you are so –

Both feel crippled.

NICK. So?

ABI. So?

NICK. So what do we do? How do we get back to – ?

Pause.

ABI. You want to?

NICK. Yeah! Fuckin' yeah.

Can we rewind or summink.

ABI. The Post-it notes?

The 'sanctions'?

NICK. Yeah.

ABI. Help me. Help me make it right.

NICK. And then?

Will we – ?

ABI. –

Enter RYAN.

RYAN. I found Wotsits. A whole family bag left over from the party. And there's Jaffa Cakes.

He gives a packet to each of them.

Have you… has anything?

The moment's gone.

I've been thinking. With my UN hat on. As you've aired your grievances I suggest we consider how we move forward.

Any thoughts?

NICK *nods.* ABI *writes on a piece of paper and hands it to* RYAN, *who reads it and passes the note to* NICK.

NICK. Thirty grand?

ABI. The deposit on our flat. Fifteen of it's mine and there's five in my ISA and I can put ten on my credit cards.

I can transfer it into my account today. It'll take two days.

We'll send that money to Irfan at Islamic Relief.

They can buy grain, helicopters and people.

They can make a difference.

We can report on that.

NICK. And bury the report on Green Crescent.

ABI. We'll tell the papers we switched supplier because they failed to deliver.

RYAN. What about Pat?

ABI. I'll tell her.

NICK. Not yet. If we can get this going, she doesn't need telling. Not till Islamic Relief are dishing out bread.

RYAN. With our brand on it.

ABI. So I'll do it.

NICK. Wait, Abs. It's your money.

You've saved for years. You'll be paying it off till you're ninety.

ABI. It's not much use now though is it?

Help me make some good come out of all this.

NICK. I'll call Irfan.

ABI. Then go and find Pat. Ryan, finish the new progress report. Whatever old ones you've got left, shred them. I'll start a plan for Islamic Relief.

Scene Six

4.19 p.m. 27th December.

PAT *enters with* NICK.

ABI *is typing at her desk.* RYAN *is typing at his desk.*

PAT. I don't know how you think that was acceptable behaviour. You can't just throw a journalist out.

NICK. The meeting room was booked.

ABI. By Nelson.

NICK. Nelson from Irrig8. You know what Nelson's like about procedure.

PAT. There was nothing on the board. I'll speak to him about that.

You're lucky Simon was so lovely. I really felt we made a
connection. You know his mother was at the same college as
Rory's wife Olivia.

He said he wouldn't make any promises. But he would try to
get a half-page.

NICK. Yeah?!

PAT. Of course, I'm sure what I said won't be worth more than
a few quotes but he did say he would jazz it up. I hardly
think we'll be front page. Page six would be fine. Just to get
the message out there.

If he can get a good photo.

NICK. That might be difficult.

PAT. I hardly think so. You don't get much better than an
earthquake.

NICK. Yeah but –

PAT. And I told him we'd send him the progress report.

ABI. Did you?

PAT. He needs the information. Apparently there's nothing on
the website for him. I'd love to know what you've actually
been doing today.

NICK. Maybe we could bullet-point some key facts?

PAT. No, let's send him the whole thing. Then he can see the
pictures, statistics, names. I don't want him making errors.

ABI. I'm not sure.

NICK. It's not quite ready yet.

PAT. But I saw Ryan collating it, on the floor.

ABI. There's a new draft.

NICK. Ryan's just proofreading it now.

RYAN *looks to* NICK *and* ABI.

PAT. What was wrong with the last one?

ABI. Erm

NICK. Stuff.

RYAN. Erm, it was me.

   I made a mistake. I spelt Pakistan wrong.

PAT. How?

RYAN. I spelt it... Plakistan.

PAT. You didn't /

NICK. He did.

   PAT *sees the bin liners full of paper.*

RYAN. So I shredded them.

   PAT *opens a bin liner.*

RYAN. I'll print them all out again. It'll look better.

PAT. I tell you how it looks, it looks like an awful waste of paper. Somewhere in the Amazon there'll be a tribe without a house because of you.

   You have so much to learn. In real work you have to be more thorough. Pay attention to the small details. We can't afford mistakes. Can we, Abi?

ABI. That's right.

RYAN. But.

PAT. No buts, just better. Work experience isn't just making tea and eating biscuits.

   PAT *enters Rory's office, keeping the door open.* ABI *goes to* NICK's *desk with a paper file in her hand – as a decoy. She checks* PAT *isn't watching and puts a piece of paper from the file down on* NICK's *desk.* ABI *indicates that* NICK *should join her.* NICK *walks over, one eye on* PAT.

ABI (*sotto voce*). So? What did Islamic Relief say?

NICK. Yeah yeah. They're on the road to Muzaffarabad and can do it.

ABI. When?

NICK. Soon as your money's through.

ABI. But it takes two days.

NICK. That's too long.

ABI. We have to hold our nerve.

NICK. It seemed like a good plan an hour ago. Now Pat's back it seems just as shit as funding terrorists.

   NICK *holds out his hand. It's shaking.*

   Look at it... I can't deal with this. I don't have the framework to cope with this sort of stuff. I'm a fundamentally simple person. I like chips and cheddar and drinking Foster's. I am a very [straight] person...

ABI. Listen, Islamic Relief will use the money to buy grain.

   Maybe we can't say we were out first or that we're leading or that we're better than anyone else. But we're helping.

   Concentrate on that.

NICK. But what do I tell the papers? Simon Cotterall's got no story now. It's just our normal day's work.

ABI. Say nothing. The media will move on. Some idiot in UKIP will have sex with a lamp post and the earthquake will disappear.

NICK. Lord, bring down another disaster. And make thousands of people die.

   ABI*'s desk phone rings.*

ABI. We're nearly done.

NICK. Are we?

   RYAN *picks up* ABI*'s phone just before she gets there.*

RYAN. Hello, Disasters Relief. Yes. (*Reply.*) Yes, she's here.

   ABI *gestures 'Of course I'm here.'*

   Who can I say is calling? (*Reply.*)

   RYAN *puts the call on hold.*

ABI. Who is it?

RYAN. It's Bastian Ridley.

ABI. Can you transfer it over?

PAT. Is that Bastian? Can I speak to him first?

ABI. I think it's quite urgent, isn't it, Ryan?

RYAN. Uh yeah.

PAT. It can't be that urgent. I want to thank him for passing on the contact.

ABI. He's flying back any minute so –

PAT. Then I'll wish him a good flight.

    201, Ryan.

ABI. S'all right, I'll let him know. 202, Ryan.

PAT. Okay fine.

    RYAN *looks to* PAT, *then* ABI.

ABI. 202.

    RYAN *begins punching the digits.* ABI *sits, relaxing.*

PAT. No, I should speak to him.

ABI. Pat, but /

PAT. You can have him all to yourself when I'm finished.

    (*To* RYAN.) 201 please, Ryan.

    RYAN *looks to* ABI, *then* NICK *then* PAT. PAT *looks expectantly at* RYAN, *growing increasingly annoyed.*

    201.

    RYAN *replaces the receiver and transfers the call to* PAT. NICK *looks desperately to* ABI. PAT's *phone rings and she picks it up. As she talks,* NICK *gets* RYAN's *attention and signals to* RYAN *that he should unplug* PAT's *phone.* RYAN *takes an age to catch on but eventually gets onto his hands and knees and begins pulling up cables and unplugging*

plugs from the extension lead under PAT'*s desk. The fan*
stops. The TV turns off. ABI'*s computer turns off. Phones*
starts falling off desks. The fan falls off the cabinet.

Bastian! Hello, yes, hello, how are you? Well I'm fine, thank
you, very well. You might see little me in a certain national
newspaper tomorrow. Oh you're still in Karachi? I'm sure I
can save you a copy – (*Replies that he is in the affected*
area.) And how are things there? (*Reply.*) Yes. Yes. We've
seen the pictures. It's – (*Reply.*) I know. We've done what we
can. (*Short reply.*) Yes, I wanted to thank you for the contact
at Green Crescent. (*Reply.*) Yes? But you told Abi – (*Reply.*
Looks at ABI.) When? And what did you? (*Long reply.*) Oh.
(*Reply. Puts her hand over her mouth.*) No, she didn't.

You've had it confirmed? (*Reply.*)

But we used him. (*Reply.*) No, no don't do that. Please, I –
(*Reply.*)

PAT *looks at* ABI.

Yes of course you've no choice.

Bye.

PAT *hangs up. She straightens some papers on her desk.*
ABI *and* NICK *wait.*

(*To* ABI.) You don't need me to tell you what he said, do you?

ABI. No.

PAT (*to* NICK). Do you?

NICK *shakes his head.*

(*To* RYAN.) Do you?

RYAN *shakes his head.*

So I'm the odd one out.

RYAN *crawls back out from under the desk.*

ABI. Pat? Before you say anything /

PAT. Are you going to say that Bastian is wrong?

ABI. No but – ?

PAT. I don't really know what you need to say then.

ABI. To explain. How we're putting it right with Islamic Relief. I've sent my own money as a donation to buy grain and I'm writing a report / and

PAT. It's too late. Bastian is going to the Charity Commission.

PAT slumps into a chair and looks to the floor.

We'll be shut down. We won't be able to help.

People will die.

Why didn't you tell me?

Am I too old, a joke? I'm not a joke.

Long pause. The others don't know what to do.

NICK. Pat?

PAT waves NICK away.

PAT. We're over.

ABI. No, no. It might not be.

PAT. How, tell me?

ABI. If I resign. I'm to blame aren't I. He was my contact, I dealt with him, I sent him the money.

PAT. No, no, I'm your line manager, it's my responsibility. I'll call Shelagh.

ABI. But it's not your fault, Pat.

You shouldn't.

PAT. Rory won't.

ABI. I'll do it. I'll resign.

NICK. No no you can't, mate. You know what the press will do to you.

I'll resign.

PAT. I will.

ABI. I will.

RYAN. I will.

NICK, ABI *and* PAT *stop and turn to* RYAN.

Erm, I… [didn't mean]

NICK. Suppose, mate, you're still at the start of your career, with nothing to lose. You just got a bit carried away, putting dodgy info on our website.

RYAN. But /

NICK. Deleting tweets. Putting fake photos in our report. Shredding evidence.

RYAN. Wait I…

NICK. And it's work experience, mate. It's not even like a proper resignation. No one'll know. Won't even be as bad as a detention.

RYAN. It's so not fair.

NICK. You did use the word Paki. And Chink. And nigger.

RYAN *flashes a panicked look at a shocked* PAT. *Then at* ABI *for help.*

RYAN. What?

You said you were my –

(*To* NICK.) You said you'd get me a job.

(*To* ABI.) You said you'd get me a job.

I bought you Mini Cheddars.

RYAN *looks like a rabbit in the headlights.*

PAT. I don't like the sound of those words at all.

RYAN. No! Stop! Wait!

When I left school my teacher told me to make some notes.

RYAN *fetches his booklet.*

I've written down all my observations from the last week.

I've been really thorough.

ABI. Pat, don't listen to this.

NICK. Wait one minute, Slave Labour.

RYAN. You said we should all tell the truth.

ABI. But –

PAT. Let him, let's hear what Ryan has to say.

RYAN (*reads*). On arriving on Christmas Eve, neither Nick nor
Abi knew of the earthquake despite both of them being here.

Nick was wearing the same shirt as the day before.

Abi was worried about calling her fiancé.

Nick hates her fiancé.

I assumed a liaison had occurred.

My suspicions were confirmed…

RYAN *reaches under* PAT*'s desk* (*where he'd be looking for
phone wires*).

…and just now I found this.

RYAN *holds up a used condom.*

On Christmas Eve, Abi heard the truth about Abdul Salim.

She tried to hack into your account and failed.

She tried to stop the payment and failed.

She told me to delete Green Crescent from the website.

And then said add Green Crescent to the website.

Abi wrote a bogus report.

I told Nick. He hid under a desk.

Nick began a new bogus report.

I shredded the bogus report.

Nick told me to add lies to the website.

Bastian found out.

You found out and you blamed Abi and Abi blamed Nick and
Nick blamed me.

Even though it was you – (PAT.) who had rushed through the plan.

Which on Christmas Eve had been Rory's idea.

Three thousand people are dead. Khalid Bhatt is dead.

You all claim to be good people.

But who am I to say? I'm just the work experience.

NICK *and* ABI *stare at* RYAN, *open-mouthed.*

PAT *opens her hand for the book.* RYAN *gives it to her and exits.*

Scene Seven

4.30 p.m. 28th December.

NICK *sits at his desk, leafing through the* Guardian. *Enter* RYAN, *in his coat, holding three copies of the* Evening Standard.

NICK. Any joy?

RYAN. I got three. First editions.

RYAN *opens one up on page five.*

We're there, page five

NICK. Big photo, nice. They've gone with 'disgrace' as well. Good good. (*Reads.*) Not sure about 'shameful'. Bit harsh.

We've got a full house now, lad. Add those to the rest yeah.

RYAN *takes the papers and adds them to his pile.*

RYAN. I'm going to look through Third Sector and Bond.

NICK *nods, resigned. He walks to Rory's office and looks through the window in the door.*

NICK. Rory's got his sergeant-major face on. Ain't looking good.

He sees PAT *and* ABI *getting ready to exit so rushes back to his chair and picks up the paper. The door to Rory's office opens and* ABI *and* PAT *exit.*

PAT. You can come in another day and pick up your things.

ABI. I might do it now.

PAT. As you like.

Pause.

ABI. Pat, I know it won't mean much but... [I'm sorry]

PAT. All publicity's good publicity, they say. I'm not sure in this case. Perhaps the board will change their minds about winding us up. Perhaps early retirement isn't so bad.

ABI. Yeah.

PAT. Remember to give us an address to send your P45. When you've found somewhere.

ABI *nods.* PAT *exits into Rory's office.*

ABI *pulls a couple of large cardboard boxes from the stationery cupboard and puts them onto her desk and packs her belongings into them.*

NICK. That's it then.

ABI. Yeah.

NICK. I can still see some of Slave Labour's knives sticking out your back.

ABI *picks up a small yucca plant.*

ABI. Would you like Robert?

NICK. Give it to Pat. I won't be in for three months. I'm on suspension, aren't I?

I'll work till the investigation and then go back home get my *FIFA* skills polished.

Looking forward to it.

ABI. You're not are you?

NICK. Nah. Be boring. Knowing there're terrorists out there buying guns without my help.

Sorry. Not funny. Bit – [nervous]

ABI *gives the plant to* NICK.

ABI. Here. Friends.

NICK. More than friends?

RYAN *stands. It's too awkward.*

RYAN. I'm really thirsty. I need a drink of Fanta.

Exit RYAN.

ABI. I meant what I said at the party.

NICK. Did ya?

ABI. Yeah.

NICK. Me too. You didn't think I was too shit in bed then?

ABI. From what I remember, it was very nice.

NICK. Nice. Don't hold back!

ABI. Better than nice.

NICK. Truth?

ABI. No. I think it was a bit fumbly and crap.

But that's okay.

NICK. Honest from now on yeah?

ABI. Yeah.

NICK. See… I know you think I'm a twat, Abs. And maybe I am sometimes. But, despite every bit of evidence, I'm on your side. Team Abi, yeah.

ABI. Thanks.

NICK. One hundred per cent. Yours. I am your twat.

Beat.

ABI (*smiles*). Thank you.

ABI *holds her arms out to hug* NICK.

ABI *gives him a hug. It lasts a moment too long. They break slightly but they're still holding each other.* ABI *runs her fingers tenderly through the hair at the side of* NICK*'s head.* NICK *strokes* ABI*'s arm.* NICK *moves to kiss her.* ABI *kisses him. It's a bit fumbly and crap.*

Okay, I should –

NICK. Now?

ABI. It's better I go.

NICK. Abs, Abi?

Don't go.

I don't want to work here if you're not here.

ABI*'s phone rings.*

ABI. That'll be my taxi.

NICK *nods.*

NICK. Those boxes be strong enough?

ABI. Yeah, think so.

NICK. I could put some tape on the bottom.

ABI. No, it's all right.

NICK. I'll help you out with them.

ABI. No, I'll take them.

NICK. Abs?

ABI. It's okay. You don't need to interfere. I'll manage.

NICK *then picks up the other box and stacks it on top.*

Bye then.

NICK. Yeah. I'll call you.

Have a cheeky pint some time. Soon.

ABI. In a week or two. When we're not colleagues any more.

Maybe go camping. Properly.

ABI *moves to the exit.*

NICK. I'll follow you.

On Twitter.

Exit ABI.

NICK *sits at his desk and puts his head in his hands. He turns his computer off. The Windows shutdown tune sounds. It's almost like this noise is the final demotivating straw. He runs his hand over the yucca-plant leaf tenderly.*

He goes to one of the filing cabinets and takes out a Ribena bottle of green gunk. It's Chris Symonds's courgette moonshine. He pours it into a glass and drinks it. It's disgusting.

Enter RYAN *with a can of Fanta and a packet of* NICK*'s favourite Mini Cheddars.* RYAN *holds out the Mini Cheddars.*

RYAN. We didn't have salt and vinegar but there was Branston Pickle. I didn't know if you liked Branston Pickle but I thought after everything that's happened it wouldn't be the worst chance to take.

It's like a peace offering.

Cos

I'm sorry for being… acting.

NICK. Like a slippery-snake-in-the-grass knobjockey.

RYAN. Yeah.

NICK. You got Brian's job though. No more being the work experience.

RYAN. Intern.

I haven't got a start date yet. But Pat said it'll probably be next Monday. If we're still going.

NICK. You'll like it here. Pat's actually a very fair boss.

RYAN. But… you know.

NICK. No, don't worry about it, mate. You've shown you've got a spine, a ruthless streak, it's what you need in this industry. You'll go far. You'll probably be employing me in years to come.

RYAN. Ha, no.

NICK gives him a quizzical look.

I don't mean that like – ! I meant 'No, I'm unlikely to be your boss' not 'I'd never employ you'.

NICK. Relax, mate, it's cool.

Here, let's celebrate your full-time employment.

NICK fetches another glass and fills both up to the top with the moonshine and hands the glass to RYAN.

Cheers.

RYAN smiles nervously.

Down the hatch.

They both drink the moonshine. When RYAN stops halfway, NICK indicates that he should finish. Both finish their drinks.

Right, I'm chuffing off home.

NICK puts his coat on. He picks up the Mini Cheddars.

I'll take these for the Tube.

NICK moves to exit.

See you tomorrow, Ryan.

RYAN. Bright and early.

Joke.

NICK flicks RYAN the Vs, smiles wryly and exits.

RYAN walks around the office. He stops at ABI's desk. He runs his fingers over the top of the PC monitor, desk, etc. As he does, the phone on ABI's desk rings. He stops, considers answering it. The phone continues to ring. He picks up the phone.

Hello, Disasters Relief? (*Reply.*) No, she's not here. She's…
erm… I could ask someone here to call you back. (*Reply.*)
Who shall I say is calling? Was that Khalid Bhatt? How do
you spell Khalid? (*Reply.*)

RYAN *finds a pen and writes down the name on a piece of
paper.*

Oh yeah, we thought you were –

So we –

I'll let them know you're safe. And you've got tent supplies.

Okay. I'll do that. Yeah.

RYAN *hangs up.* RYAN *picks the Post-it note up and
considers it. He scrunches it up and throws it into the bin.
He considers. Then picks it out, smoothes it out and sticks it
on* PAT's *monitor.*

*He settles into the seat, getting comfortable, beginning to
own the space. Victorious.*

End.

www.nickhernbooks.co.uk

facebook.com/nickhernbooks

twitter.com/nickhernbooks